CHAMPLAIN

CHAMPLAIN

By N. E. Dionne

UNIVERSITY OF TORONTO PRESS
1963

Copyright, Canada, 1963
by University of Toronto Press
Reprinted in paperback 2015

ISBN 978-0-8020-6013-6 (paper)

PUBLISHER'S NOTE

This standard general biography of Champlain, the founder of Canada, was issued previously in the famous Makers of Canada Series, which is now out of print, although still in frequent use in libraries. This is the first time any of the volumes has been published separately from the complete set.

N. E. Dionne, F.R.S.C., was a noted French-Canadian historian and bibliographer (1848-1917). He served as editor of *Le Courrier du Canada* for twelve years, and in 1892 was appointed head of the Quebec Legislative Library. He published a large number of historical works, the best known of which are his studies of Cartier and Champlain, and his four-volume *Inventaire chronologique*, an indispensable bibliography of the province of Quebec.

Champlain was revised in 1926 by Ralph Flenley, Professor of History at the University of Toronto.

INTRODUCTION

IN undertaking to write a biography of Samuel Champlain, the founder of Quebec and the father of New France, our only design is to make somewhat better known the dominant characteristics of the life and achievements of a man whose memory is becoming more cherished as the years roll on.

Every one will admire Champlain's disinterested actions, his courage, his loyalty, his charity, and all those noble and magnificent qualities which are rarely found united in one individual in so prominent a degree. We cannot overpraise that self-abnegation which enabled him to bear without complaint the ingratitude of many of his interpreters, and the servants of the merchants; nor can we overlook, either, the charity which he exercised towards the aborigines and new settlers; the protection which he afforded them under trying circumstances, or his zeal in promoting the honour and glory of God, and his respect for the Récollet and Jesuit fathers who honoured him with their cordial friendship. His wisdom is evidenced in such a practical fact as his choice of Quebec as the capital of New France, despite the rival claims of Montreal and Three Rivers, and his numerous writings reveal him to us as a keen and sagacious

INTRODUCTION

observer, a man of science and a skilful and intrepid mariner. As a cosmographer, Champlain added yet another laurel to his crown, for he excelled all his predecessors, both by the ample volume of his descriptions and by the logical arrangement of the geographical data which he supplied. The impetus which he gave to cartographical science can scarcely be overestimated.

Naturalist, mariner, geographer, such was Samuel Champlain, and to a degree remarkable for the age in which he lived. It is, perhaps, unnecessary to dwell upon the morality of the virtuous founder. The testimony of the Hurons, who, twenty years after his death, still pointed to the life of Champlain as a model of all Christian virtues, is sufficient, and it is certain that no governor under the old régime presented a more brilliant example of faith, piety, uprightness, or soundness of judgment. A brief outline of the character of Champlain has been given in order that the plan of this biography may be better understood. Let us now glance at his career more in detail.

Before becoming the founder of colonies, Champlain entered the French army, where he devoted himself to the religion of his ancestors. This was the first important step in his long and eventful career. A martial life, however, does not appear to have held out the same inducements as that of a mariner. An opportunity was presented which enabled him to gratify his tastes, when the Spanish government

INTRODUCTION

sent out an armada to encounter the English in the Gulf of Mexico. Champlain was given the command of a ship in this expedition, but his experience during the war served rather as an occasion to develop his genius as a mariner and cosmographer, than to add to his renown as a warrior.

God, who in His providence disposes of the lives of men according to His divine wisdom, directed the steps of Champlain towards the shores of the future New France. If the mother country had not completely forgotten this land of ours, discovered by one of her greatest captains, she had, at least, neglected it. The honour of bringing the king's attention to this vast country, which was French by the right of discovery, was reserved for the modest son of Brouage.

While Pierre du Gua, Sieur de Monts, was wasting his years and expending large sums of money in his fruitless efforts to colonize the island of Ste. Croix and Port Royal, Champlain's voyage to Acadia and his discovery of the New England coast were practically useful, and in consequence Champlain endeavoured to assure de Monts that his own efforts would be more advantageously directed to the shores of the St. Lawrence, for here it was obvious that the development of the country must commence.

Champlain's next step was to found Quebec. With this act began our colonial history, the foundation of a Canadian people with its long line

INTRODUCTION

of heroic characters distinguished by their simplicity and by their adherence to the faith of their fathers. Quebec was founded, but nothing more was accomplished at the moment owing to the lack of means. The trials of Champlain now commenced. Day by day he had to contend against his own countrymen. The attractions of fur trading were too great for the merchants to induce them to settle down and develop the country around them, and they were unwilling to fulfil their promises or to act in accordance with the terms of their patents.

During the next twenty years Champlain crossed the ocean eighteen times. Each voyage was made in the interest of the colony, and he sought by every means in his power, by prayers and petitions, to obtain the control of the commerce of the country so as to make it beneficial to all. In spite of his extraordinary exertions and the force of his will, he foresaw the fatal issue of his labours.

The settlers were few in number, bread and provisions were scarce, and the condition of the infant colony was truly deplorable. At this distressing period a British fleet arrived in the harbour of Quebec. What was to be done ? The rude fortress of St. Louis could not withstand the assault of an armed fleet, even if it were well defended. But Champlain had no ammunition, and he, therefore, adopted the only course open to him of capitulating and handing over the keys of the fort to the commander, Kirke. Champlain then left Quebec and

INTRODUCTION

returned to France. Bitter was this journey to him, for it was like passing into exile to see the familiar heights of Quebec fade into the distance, the city of his foundation and the country of his adoption.

We have an idea of his sorrow during the three years that England maintained supremacy in Canada, for he says that the days were as long as months. During his enforced sojourn in France, Champlain exerted all his energies to revive interest in the abandoned colony. His plan was to recover the country by all means. Finally success crowned his efforts, and the treaty of St. Germain-en-Laye gave back to France the young settlement. Champlain recrossed the sea and planted the lily banner of France upon the heights of Cape Diamond.

In the year 1635 Champlain was taken ill, and died on Christmas Day, after having devoted forty years of his life to the promotion of the religion and commercial interests of the land of his ancestors, but he bequeathed to the Canadian people the priceless heritage of Quebec, and the memory of a pure and honest heart.

Before Champlain's death, however, Quebec had commenced to develop. On the Beauport coast might be seen the residences of many of the settlers who arrived from the province of Perche in 1634. On the shores of the river Lairet, the Jesuits had built a convent, where the young Indians received instruction; and agriculture had received some attention. Robert Giffard had established a colony at

INTRODUCTION

Beauport which formed the nucleus of a population in this section of the country. Near Fort St. Louis the steeple of Notre Dame de la Recouvrance gave witness that Champlain had fulfilled his promise to build a church at Quebec if the country was restored to her ancient masters.

The colony was now entering upon an era of prosperity, and that harmony and happiness which Champlain had longed for in his life, and which occupied his thoughts even in death, were destined to be realized.

N. E. D.

INTRODUCTION

NOTE BY THE REVISER

Very little has been added to our knowledge of Champlain's life since the first appearance of this biography. The main task of the reviser therefore has been to correct errors of fact or of translation, since much of the volume was first written in French, and to ensure that nothing material to the presentation of Champlain's career has been omitted. I have also added references to such English translations of Champlain's works as exist, notably to that now in course of publication by the Champlain Society. I have not attempted to modify the general point of view manifested in the biography, save where alteration seemed necessary for the true presentation of facts. Nor have I interfered with the structure or arrangement of the book, since to do this would mean writing a new biography.

RALPH FLENLEY

CONTENTS

CHAPTER I	Page
CHAMPLAIN'S FIRST VOYAGE TO AMERICA	1
CHAPTER II	
ACADIA—STE. CROIX ISLAND—PORT ROYAL	17
CHAPTER III	
THE FOUNDING OF QUEBEC	39
CHAPTER IV	
CHAMPLAIN'S VOYAGES OF 1610, 1611, 1613	59
CHAPTER V	
THE RÉCOLLETS AND THEIR MISSIONS	81
CHAPTER VI	
WAR AGAINST THE IROQUOIS, 1615	101

CONTENTS

CHAPTER VII
FUR TRADE 119

CHAPTER VIII
CHAMPLAIN, THE JESUITS AND THE SAVAGES . 143

CHAPTER IX
THE COMPANY OF NEW FRANCE OR HUNDRED ASSOCIATES 167

CHAPTER X
THE CAPITULATION OF QUEBEC, 1629 . . 187

CHAPTER XI
THE LAST EVENTS OF 1629 . . . 199

CHAPTER XII
QUEBEC RESTORED . . . 211

CHAPTER XIII
THE JESUIT MISSIONS IN NEW FRANCE . 227

CONTENTS

CHAPTER XIV   Page

THE GROWTH OF QUEBEC   243

CHAPTER XV

CONCLUSION   261

CHRONOLOGICAL APPENDIX   .   .   .   283

INDEX   289

CHAMPLAIN

CHAPTER I

CHAMPLAIN'S FIRST VOYAGE TO AMERICA

SAMUEL CHAMPLAIN, the issue of the marriage of Antoine Champlain and Marguerite Le Roy, was born at Brouage, now Hiers Brouage, a small village in the province of Saintonge, France, in the year 1570, or according to the *Biographie Sanitingeoise* in 1567.

We know practically nothing of Champlain's years in one of the most troublous periods in the history of France, that of the wars of religion. His youth appears to have glided quietly away, spent for the most part with his family, and in assisting his father, who was a mariner, in his wanderings upon the sea. The knowledge thus obtained was of great service to him, for after a while he became not only conversant with the life of a mariner, but also with the science of geography and of astronomy. When Samuel Champlain was about twenty years of age, he tendered his services to Marshal d'Aumont, one of the chief commanders of the Catholic army in its expedition against the Huguenots.

When the war was finished and the army was disbanded in 1598, Champlain returned to Brouage, and sought a favourable opportunity to advance his fortune in a manner more agreeable, if

CHAMPLAIN

possible, to his tastes, and more compatible with his abilities. In the meantime Champlain did not remain idle, for he resolved to find the means of making a voyage to Spain in order "to acquire and cultivate acquaintance," and, by a voyage to New Spain, to "make a true report to His Majesty (Henry IV) of the particularities which could not be known to any Frenchmen, for the reason that they have not free access there." He left Blavet at the beginning of the month of August, and ten days later he arrived near Cape Finisterre. Having remained for six days at the Isle of Bayona, in Galicia, he proceeded towards San Lucar de Barameda, which is at the mouth of the Guadalquivir, where he remained for three months. During this time he went to Seville and made surveys of the place. While Champlain was at Seville, *a patache*, or advice boat, arrived from Porto Rico bearing a communication addressed to the king of Spain, informing him that an English expedition had put out to sea with the intention of attacking Porto Rico. The king fitted out twenty ships to oppose the English, one of them, the *Saint Julien*, was commanded by Provençal, Champlain's uncle. Champlain proposed to join the expedition under his uncle, but the fleet did not go. Provençal was ordered elsewhere, and General Soubriago offered the command of the *Saint Julien* to Champlain, in the fleet gathered for the yearly voyage to the New World.

THE ARMADA

The armada set sail in the beginning of January, 1599, and within six days, favoured by a fresh breeze, the vessels sighted the Canary Islands. Two months and six days later the armada drew near to the island called La Désirade, which is the first island approached in this passage to the Indies. The ships anchored for the first time at Nacou, which is one of the finest ports of the Guadeloupe. After having passed Marguerite Island and the Virgins, Champlain proceeded to San Juan de Porto Rico,[1] where he found that both the town and the castle or fortress had been abandoned, and that the merchants had either made their escape or had been taken prisoners. The English army had left the town and had taken the Spanish governor with them, as he had surrendered on the condition that his life should be spared.

On leaving Porto Rico the general divided the galleons into three squadrons, and retained four vessels under his own command. Three were sent to Porto Bello, and three, including Champlain's vessel, to New Spain. Champlain arrived at Saint Jean de Luz, fully four hundred leagues from

[1] This island is only forty leagues in length and twenty in breadth, and belonged to the Spanish from the date of its discovery by Ponce de León in 1509, to 1598. When Champlain visited the island it had been taken by George Clifford, Earl of Cumberland. During the same year Sir John Berkeley commanded, but being unable to remain there, he deserted the place, and joined Clifford near the Azores, when both went to England, having lost about seven hundred men during their expedition.

CHAMPLAIN

Porto Rico. This place later was given the name of San Juan d'Ulloa. Fifteen days afterwards we find Champlain setting out for Mexico, situated at a distance of two hundred miles from San Juan.

Champlain was evidently very much interested in this country, and his description is that of an enthusiast: "It is impossible to see or desire a more beautiful country than this kingdom of New Spain, which is three hundred leagues in length and two hundred in breadth. . . . The whole of this country is ornamented with very fine rivers and streams . . . the land is very fertile, producing corn twice in the year . . . the trees are never devoid of fruit and are always green." The journey to Mexico occupied a month and Champlain gave an animated description of the city of Mexico, of its superb palaces, temples, houses and buildings, and well laid streets, as well as of the surrounding country.

After leaving Mexico, Champlain returned to San Juan de Luz, and from there sailed in a *patache* to Porto Bello, "the most evil and unhealthy residence in the world." The harbour, however, was good and well fortified. From Porto Bello to Panama, which is on the sea, the distance is only seventeen leagues, and it is interesting to read Champlain's description:—

"One may judge that if the four leagues of land which there are from Panama to this river were cut

THE PANAMA ROUTE

through, one might pass from the South Sea to the ocean on the other side, and thus shorten the route by more than fifteen hundred leagues; and from Panama to the Straits of Magellan would be an island, and from Panama to the New-found-lands would be another island, so that the whole of America would be in two islands."

It is thus seen that the idea of connecting the Atlantic ocean with the Pacific by cutting through the Isthmus of Panama is not a modern one, as it was promulgated by Champlain over three hundred years ago.

At this time Spain was in great need of a good transportation service at the isthmus. The treasures of Peru were sent to Europe by the Panama route to Porto Bello, from where the ships sailed to the old continent. The route between the Pacific coast and the Gulf of Mexico was exceedingly bad. Sometimes the merchants forwarded European goods to Panama, having them transported to Chagres. Here they were landed in boats and conveyed to Cruces. From Cruces to Panama mules were employed for the remainder of the journey. It was, however, the route taken by travellers visiting Peru, Chili, New Granada, Venezuela, and other Spanish possessions on the Pacific coast. The most regular connection between the two oceans was from Fort Acapulco to Vera Cruz, through Mexico. If Spain had adopted a better line of communication with her western territories in the New World

CHAMPLAIN

she might have derived vast treasure from that source. In the year 1551 Lopez de Gomara, the author of a "History of Indies," a work written with care and displaying considerable erudition, proposed to unite the two oceans by means of canals at three different points, Chagres, Nicaragua and Tehuantepec. Gomara's proposals were not acted upon, and the honour of designing the project was reserved for France. Ferdinand de Lesseps, who succeeded in connecting the Mediterranean Sea with the Red Sea, was the man who, after the lapse of centuries, seriously interested his fellow-countrymen in boring the Isthmus of Panama.

Champlain returned to San Juan de Luz, where he remained for fifteen days, and he then proceeded to Havana, the rendezvous of the army and of the fleet. Eighteen days later he embarked in a vessel bound for Cartagena, where there was a good port, sheltered from all winds. Upon his return to Havana Champlain met his general and spent four months in collecting valuable information relating to the interesting island of Cuba. From Havana he proceeded past the Bahama channel, approached Bermuda Island, Terceira, one of the Azores, and sighted Cape St. Vincent, where he captured two armed English vessels, which were taken to Seville.

Champlain returned to France in March, 1601, having been absent on his first voyage for a period of two years and two months, during which time he collected much valuable information. He also wrote

HIS FIRST VOYAGE

a small volume containing plans, maps and engravings, fairly well executed for the time. The manuscript of this volume is still preserved; it covers one hundred and fifteen pages with sixty-two drawings, coloured and surrounded with blue and yellow lines. It appears to have been written between 1601 and 1603.[1]

The first voyage of Champlain across the Atlantic, though important from a military standpoint, did not suffice to satisfy the ambition of a man whose thoughts were bent upon discovery and colonization. Champlain was a navigator by instinct, and in his writings he gave to nautical science the first place.

"Of all the most useful and excellent arts," he writes, "that of navigation has always seemed to me to occupy the first place. For the more hazardous it is, the greater the perils and losses by which it is attended, so much the more is it esteemed and exalted above all others, being wholly unsuited to

[1] This volume is entitled *Brief Discours des choses plus remarquables que Samuel Champlain de Brouage A reconneues aux Indes Occidentalles Au voiage qu'il en a faict icelles en l'année V•IIIJ. XXIX, et en l'année VI•J, comme ensuit.*

This manuscript was discovered by M. Féret, antiquarian, poet and librarian, of Dieppe. The Hakluyt Society had it translated in 1859, and published at London. In 1870 the Reverend Laverdière, librarian of the Laval University, of Quebec, had it printed in French, with the designs, coloured for the most part, with the complete works of Champlain. It is also printed (with translation) in the Champlain Society's edition of *The Works of Samuel de Champlain*, edited by H. P. Biggar: Toronto, 1922. This manuscript is supposed to have been preserved by a collateral descendant of Aymar de Chastes.

the timid and irresolute. By this art we obtain a knowledge of different countries, regions and realms. By it we attract and bring to our own land all kinds of riches; by it the idolatry of Paganism is over-thrown and Christianity proclaimed throughout all the regions of the earth. This is the art which won my love in my early years and induced me to expose myself almost all my life to the impetuous waves of the ocean, and led me to explore the coasts of a portion of America, especially those of New France, where I have always desired to see the lily flourish, together with the only religion, Catholic, Apostolic and Roman."

After his return to France in the year 1601, Champlain received a pension, together with the appointment of geographer to the king. Pierre de Chauvin, Sieur de Tontuit, who had unsuccessfully endeavoured to establish a settlement at Tadousac, died at this time, while Champlain was residing in Paris. Here he had the good fortune to meet Aymar de Chastes, governor of the town and château of Dieppe, under whose orders he had served during the latter years of the war with the League.

De Chastes, who had resolved to undertake the colonization of Canada, obtained a commission from the king, and formed a company, composed of several gentlemen and the principal merchants of Rouen. François Gravé, Sieur du Pont, who had already accompanied Chauvin to Tadousac, was

SIEUR DE CHASTES

chosen to return there and to examine the Sault St. Louis and the country beyond.

"Going from time to time to see the Sieur de Chastes," writes Champlain, "judging that I might serve him in his design, he did me the honour to communicate something of it to me, and asked me if it would be agreeable to me to make the voyage, to examine the country, and to see what those engaged in the undertaking should do. I told him that I was very much his servant, but that I could not give myself license to undertake the voyage without the commands of the king, to whom I was bound, as well by birth as by the pension with which His Majesty honoured me to enable me to maintain myself near his person, but that, if it should please him to speak to the king about it, and give me his commands, that it should be very agreeable to me, which he promised and did, and received the king's orders for me to make the voyage and make a faithful report thereof; and for that purpose M. de Gesvres, secretary of his commandments, sent me with a letter to the said Du Pont-Gravé, desiring him to take me in his ship and enable me to see and examine what could be done in the country, giving me every possible assistance."

"*Me violà expédié*," says Champlain, "I leave Paris and take passage on Pont-Gravé's ship in the year 1603, the 15th of the month of March." The voyage was favourable for the first fifteen days, but

CHAMPLAIN

on the 30th a heavy storm arose, "more thunder than wind," which lasted until April 16th. On May 6th the vessel approached Newfoundland, and arrived at Tadousac[1] on the 24th. Here they met with about one hundred Indians, under the command of Anadabijou, who were rejoicing on account of their recent victory over the Iroquois. The chief made a long harangue, speaking slowly. He congratulated himself upon his friendship with the French nation, and stated that he was happy to learn that the king was anxious to send some of his subjects to reside in the country and to assist them in their wars. Champlain was also informed that the Etchemins, the Algonquins, and the Montagnais, to the number of about one thousand, had lately been engaged in warfare with the Iroquois, whom they had vanquished with the loss of one hundred men.

On June 9th following, Champlain witnessed the spectacle of a grand feast given by the Indians in commemoration of their victory. The celebration consisted of dances, songs, speeches and games. Tessouat, the *sagamo* of the Ottawas, was the chief captain, and took a prominent part in the demonstration.

After a long description of these public festivities, Champlain gives ample details of the manners

---

[1] Tadousac means *breast*, and is derived from the Montagnais *Totouchac*. Father Jérôme Lalemant says that the Indians called the place *Sadilege*.

INDIAN SUPERSTITIONS

and customs of the Indians, especially of their superstitions. The Indians believed that a God existed who was the creator of all things, but they had a curious manner of explaining the creation of man. "When God had made everything," they said, "He took a quantity of arrows and fixed them in the earth, whence came men and women, who have increased ever since." The *sagamo* said they believed in the existence of a God, a son, a mother and a sun; that God was the greatest of the four; that the son and the sun were both good; that the mother was a lesser person, and of no value; the father was none too good.

The Indians were convinced that their deity had held communication with their ancestors. One day five Indians ran towards the setting sun where they met God, who asked them, "Where are you going?" "We are going to seek a living," they replied. Then God said, "You will find it here." But they did not hear the divine word, and went away. Then God took a stone and touched two of them, and they were immediately turned into stones. Addressing the three other Indians, God asked the same question, "Where are you going?" and He was given the same answer. "Do not go further," said the divine voice, "you will find your living here." Seeing nothing, however, they continued their journey. Then God took two sticks and touched two of them, and they were at once turned into sticks. The fifth Indian, however, paused, and God

CHAMPLAIN

gave him some meat, which he ate, and he afterwards returned to his countrymen.

These Indian tribes had their jugglers, whom they called *pilotois*, from the Basques, or *autmoins*, which means a magician. These jugglers exercised great sway over the Indians, who would not hesitate to kill a Frenchman if the jugglers decided that it was necessary.

In spite of their superstitions Champlain believed that it would be an easy task to convert the Indians to Christianity, especially if the French resided near them. This desirable end was not to be attained without great difficulty, as Champlain soon realized, for the missionaries toiled for many years before their efforts were crowned with success.

Champlain now proceeded to explore the river Saguenay for a distance of twelve to fifteen leagues, and he thus describes the scenery:—

"All the land I have seen is composed of rocks, covered with fir woods, cypress, birch, very unpleasing land, where I could not find a league of level land on each side." He also learned from the Indians of the existence of Lake St. John, and of a salt sea away towards the north. It was evidently Hudson Bay to which these northern tribes directed Champlain's attention, and if they had not seen it themselves they had probably heard of its existence from the Indians dwelling around the southern or south-western shores of the bay, who

FURTHER EXPLORATIONS, 1603

came annually to Nemiscau Lake to trade their furs. This lake was half way between Hudson Bay and the river St. Lawrence. The Kilistinons and other Indians of the north had regular communication with their *congénères* scattered along the shores of the St. Maurice and the several rivers which flow into Lake St. John.

When the French arrived in Canada with Chauvin, in the year 1600, they began to monopolize the fur trade of all the Indian nations, but some years later the English established themselves on the shores of Hudson Bay, and prosecuted the trade for their own benefit.

Champlain could not, evidently, have been in possession of any exact information as to the existence of this large bay, as he was searching for a northern passage to Cathay, the great *desideratum* of all the navigators and explorers of the time.

After having promised to aid the various tribes gathered at Tadousac in their wars, Champlain and Pont-Gravé proceeded to Sault St. Louis. This expedition lasted fifteen days, in which they reached Hare Island, so named by Jacques Cartier, and the Island of Orleans. The ship anchored at Quebec where Champlain stopped to make a short investigation of the country watered by the St. Lawrence, and they then proceeded to Sault St. Louis. Here Champlain gathered much valuable information relating to lakes Ontario and Erie, the Detroit River, Niagara Falls, and the rapids of the St. Lawrence.

CHAMPLAIN

Returning to Tadousac, he determined to explore Gaspesia, and proceeded to visit Percé and Mal Bay, where he met Indians at every turn. He also was informed by Prévert, from St. Malo, who was exploring the country, of the existence of a copper mine.

Champlain carefully noted all the information he had received, and after his return to Tadousac he sailed again for France on August 16th, 1603, and reached Havre de Grâce, after a passage of thirty-five days. On his arrival in France, he heard that Aymar de Chastes had died a few weeks previously, on August 13th. This was a great loss to Canada, and especially to Champlain, for he was convinced that the noble and enterprising de Chastes was seriously disposed to colonize New France. "In this enterprise," he says, "I cannot find a single fault, because it has been well inaugurated." With the death of de Chastes, the project of colonizing would undoubtedly have fallen through had not Champlain been present to promote another movement in this direction. Champlain had an interview with the king, and presented him with a map of the country which he had visited, and placed in his hands a relation of his voyage.[1] Henry IV was so favourably im-

---

[1] This volume is entitled *Des Sauvages ou Voyage de Samuel Champlain de Brouage, fait en la Nouvelle France, l'an mil six cent trois* . . . . *A Paris . . . 1604.*

Extremely rare. Copies are to be found in the British Museum,

A RARE VOLUME

pressed that he promised to assist Champlain in his patriotic designs.

the Bibliothèque Nationale and the Bibliothèque Sainte-Geneviève at Paris.

This volume contains a dedication to Charles de Montmorency, admiral of France, a letter in verse from the Sieur de la Franchise, and an extract from the *Privilège du Roi*, dated November 15th, 1603, signed by Brigard.

The second edition does not differ much from the preceding, and its title bears the date 1604. Purchas's *Pilgrims* contains an English version of this last edition. We find a synopsis of it in the *Mercure François*, 1609, in the preface to the former called *Chronologie Septennaire de l'Histoire de la paix entre les rois de France et d'Espagne, 1598-1608*. This historical part has been borrowed by Victor Palma Cayet for Champlain's Voyage, and its title is: *Navigation des Français en la Nouvelle France dite Canada*.

The *Des Sauvages* is reprinted, from the original texts, and with the addition of an English translation by H. H. Langton, in vol i. of the Champlain Society's edition of *The Works of Samuel de Champlain*, edited by H. P. Biggar: Toronto, 1922.

CHAPTER II

ACADIA—STE. CROIX ISLAND—PORT ROYAL

SOON after the period mentioned at the close of the previous chapter, Pierre du Gua, Sieur de Monts, Governor of Pons, a native of the ancient province of Saintonge, who had served under Henry IV, obtained a commission as "Lieutenant genéral au pays de Cadie, du 40° au 46°," on the condition that his energies should be especially directed to the propagation of the Catholic faith.

De Monts was a Huguenot; nevertheless he agreed to take with him to America a number of Catholic priests, and to see that they were respected and obeyed. Champlain was not satisfied with the choice of a Protestant to colonize a country which he had intended to make solely Catholic, and he states, "that those enterprises made hastily never succeed."

De Monts was not a stranger to America. He had first visited the country with Chauvin in 1600, but when he left Tadousac he was so discouraged that he determined, in the event of his becoming master of the situation, to attempt colonization only in Acadia, or on the eastern borders of the continent running towards Florida.

It was well known in France that Acadia was

CHAMPLAIN

the richest and most fertile part of the New World. Excellent harbours and good soil were found there. Fish abounded near its coasts; its forests were numerous and dense. An opinion existed that there were numerous mines, rich in copper, coal and gypsum. This country was also the favourite of the Normans, Bretons and Basques, who for a hundred years had pursued their callings as fishermen or traders without interruption.

De Monts, however, was unable to bear the expense of this undertaking alone, and he consequently formed a company, composed of merchants of Rouen, La Rochelle and other towns. To further the enterprise Henry IV diminished the duty on merchandises exported from Acadia and Canada, and granted to the company the exclusive privilege of fur trading for a period of ten years, "from Cape de Raze to the 40°, comprising all the Acadian coast, Cape Breton, Baie des Chaleurs, Percé Island, Gaspé, Chisedec, Miramichi, Tadousac and Canada River, from either side, and all the bays and rivers which flow within these shores."

Acadia of that day was not confined to the peninsula of our own time, called Nova Scotia. It included that part of the continent which extends from the river St. John to the Penobscot. These boundaries were the cause of long quarrels and fierce and bloody wars between England and France until they were finally settled by the Treaty of Utrecht. In the early part of April, 1604, the king's proc-

DE MONTS' COMPANY

lamation confining the fur trade to de Monts and his associates was published in every harbour of France. Four ships were lying at anchor at Havre de Grâce, ready to sail, and one hundred and twenty passages had been secured in two of the ships. Pont-Gravé commanded one of the vessels of one hundred and twenty tons burthen, and another vessel of one hundred and fifty tons was under the charge of de Monts, who had taken on board Jean de Biencourt, Sieur de Poutrincourt, a gentleman of Picardy, Samuel Champlain, some Catholic priests and some Protestant ministers. Poutrincourt was going to America with the intention of residing there with his family. He was a good Catholic and a loyal subject. Champlain was attached to de Monts' expedition as geographer and historian.

The rendezvous had been fixed at Canseau, but de Monts proceeded directly to Port au Mouton on the Acadian coast, where he decided to await the arrival of Pont-Gravé. In the meantime Champlain explored the country from Port au Mouton to Port Sainte Marguerite, now called St. Mary's Bay. This occupied a whole month. He also named Cape Négré, Cape Fourchu and Long Island. Champlain reported to de Monts that St. Mary's Bay was a suitable place to establish a settlement, and, following this advice, the lieutenant-general proceeded with Champlain to this bay, and further explored the Bay of Fundy, or French Bay. They soon perceived the entrance to another splendid port, which is now known as Annapolis Bay, or Port Royal.

Notwithstanding the authority of Lescarbot, Champlain was the first to give this place the name of Port Royal, for he says himself, "I have named this harbour Port Royal." When de Monts named the place La Baie Française, Champlain did not hesitate to give to his chief the credit which he deserved.

Three rivers flow into this splendid harbour: the Rivière de l'Equille, so called from a little fish of the size of our *éperlan* or *lançon*, which is found there in large quantities; the river named St. Antoine by Champlain, and a stream called de la Roche by Champlain, and de l'Orignac by Lescarbot.

After having explored the harbour, Champlain traversed La Baie Francaise to see whether he could discover the copper mine mentioned by Prévert of St. Malo, and he soon arrived at a place which he named the Cape of Two Bays, or Chignecto, and perceived the High Islands, where a copper mine was found.

On May 20th an expedition started from the Port of Mines, in search of a place suitable for a permanent settlement. Proceeding towards the south-west they stopped at the entrance of a large river, which was named St. John, as it was on St. John's day that they arrived there. The savages called the river Ouigoudi. "This river is danger-

ISLAND OF STE. CROIX

ous," writes Champlain, "if one does not observe carefully certain points and rocks on the two sides. It is so narrow at its entrance and then becomes broader. A certain point being passed it becomes narrower again, and forms a kind of fall between two large cliffs, where the water runs so rapidly that a piece of wood thrown in is drawn under and not seen again. But by waiting till high tide you can pass this fall very easily. Then it expands again to the extent of about a league in some places where there are three islands."

Champlain did not explore the river further, but he ascertained a few days later that the Indians used the river in their journeys to Tadousac, making but a short portage on the way.

As preparations had shortly to be made for winter quarters, de Monts decided to proceed southwards, and the party at length came to a number of islands at the entrance of the river Ste. Croix, or Des Etchemins. One of these islands was chosen for their establishment, and named Ste. Croix, "because," says Lescarbot, "they perceived two leagues above this island two streams flowing into the channel of the river, presenting the appearance of a cross." De Monts at once commenced to fortify the place by forming a barricade on a little islet, which served as a station on which he set up a cannon; it was situated halfway between the mainland and the island of Ste. Croix. Some days afterwards all the French who were waiting in St. Mary's Bay disembarked on the island. They were all eager and willing to work, and commenced to render the place habitable. They erected a storehouse and a residence for de Monts, and built an oven and a handmill for grinding wheat. Some gardens were also laid out, and various kinds of seeds were sown, which flourished well on the mainland, though not on the island, which was too sandy.

De Monts was anxious to ascertain the location of a mine of pure copper which had been spoken of, and accordingly he despatched Champlain, with a savage named Messamouet, who asserted that he could find the place. At about eight leagues from the island, near the river St. John, they found a mine of copper, which, however, was not pure, though fairly good. According to the report of the miner, it would yield about eighteen per cent. Lescarbot says that amidst the rocks, diamonds and some blue and clear stones could be found as precious as turquoises. Champdoré, one of the carpenters, took one of these stones to France, and had it divided into many fragments and mounted by an artist. De Monts and Poutrincourt, to whom they were presented, considered these gems so valuable that they offered them to the king. A goldsmith offered Poutrincourt fifteen crown pieces for one of them.

Agriculture did not flourish on the island of Ste. Croix, which is about half a league in circumference. The rays of the sun parched the sand so that

RAVAGES OF SCURVY

the gardens were entirely unproductive, and there was a complete dearth of water. At the commencement there was a fair quantity of wood, but when the buildings were finished there was scarcely any left; the inhabitants, consequently, nearly perished from cold in the winter. All the liquor, wine and beer became frozen, and as there was no water the people were compelled to drink melted snow. A malignant epidemic of scurvy broke out, and of seventy-nine persons thirty-five died from the disease and more than twenty were at the point of death.

This disease proved one of the obstacles to rapid colonization in New France. It was epidemic, contagious and often fatal. It is a somewhat remarkable fact that the epidemic was prevalent amongst the French only when they were established on the soil, being rarely discovered on ship-board. Jacques Cartier had experienced the horrors of this disease in the winter of 1535-6, when out of his one hundred and ten men twenty-five died, and only three or four remained altogether free from attack. During the year 1542-3, Roberval saw fifty persons dying of the disease at Charlesbourg Royal. At Ste. Croix the proportion of deaths was still greater, thirty-five out of seventy-nine. There was a physician attached to de Monts' party, but he did not understand the disease, and therefore could not satisfactorily prescribe for it. De Monts also consulted many physicians in Paris, but he did not receive answers that were of much service to him.

CHAMPLAIN

At the commencement of the seventeenth century scientific men distinguished scurvy on land from scurvy on sea. They laboured under the false impression that the one differed from the other. Champlain called the disease *mal de terre*. It is certain, however, that the symptoms did not vary in either case, as we may ascertain from the descriptions furnished by Jacques Cartier and Champlain.

The position of the settlement was soon proved to be untenable, and de Monts was certainly to blame for this unhappy state of affairs. Why did he abandon Port Royal, where he had found abundant water? Champlain, however, defends the action of his chief.

"It would be very difficult," he says, "to ascertain the character of this region without spending a winter in it, for, on arriving here in summer, everything is very agreeable in consequence of the woods, fine country, and the many varieties of good fish which are found." We must not forget, however, that the climate of this island differed very little from that of Tadousac, which had greatly disappointed de Monts, and that his sole object in settling in a more southern latitude was to avoid the disagreeable consequences of the climate.

Champlain made a plan of the island of Ste. Croix, indicating the buildings constructed for the habitation of the settlers. We observe many isolated

PLAN OF STE. CROIX

tenements forming a large square. On one side was the residence of Champlain, of Champdoré and d'Orville, with a large garden opposite. Near d'Orville's residence was a small building set apart for the missionaries. On the other side may be seen the storehouse, de Monts' dwelling, a public hall where the people spent their leisure, and a building for Boulay and the workmen. In an angle of the large square were the residences of Genestou, Sourin, de Beaumont, La Motte, Bourioli and Fougeray. A small fort is shown at one end of the island, approached by a pathway. The chapel of the priest Aubry was located near the cannon of the fort. Such was the plan of the first Acadian settlement. Much expense had been incurred for a very poor result.

De Monts was the directing spirit of the colony, and in spite of his noble attempts, he realized that his efforts were fruitless and that he would have to try another place for a permanent settlement. By the direction of his chief, Champlain accordingly had already explored the seacoast of Norumbega.

De Monts has found a defender in Moreau, who held that Ste. Croix was only intended for winter quarters. If this had been his intention, we can scarcely believe that he would have incurred so great an expense in building a number of houses. Lescarbot, whose testimony is most valuable, says: "When we go into a country to take possession of

CHAMPLAIN

land we don't stop on islands to imprison ourselves. If that island had been supplied with rivers or streams, if the soil had been favourable to agriculture, it would have been half wrong." But this island lacked the very first element essential to life, fresh water.

Towards the middle of May, 1605, every one's attention was directed towards France, as the ships which had been expected for over a month had not yet arrived. De Monts then determined to send his party to Gaspé in two large boats to get passage to France. At this juncture, however, Pont-Gravé arrived at Ste. Croix with his crew, comprising forty men.

De Monts and Pont-Gravé held a consultation and decided to seek a more suitable place for a settlement, rather than to return to France. De Monts was still under the impression that the best plan was to attempt to settle in the vicinity of Florida, although the result of Champlain's exploration along the coast of the Norumbega[1] was considered unsatisfactory.

Let us now examine what Champlain had accomplished during the month of September, 1604.

He left Ste. Croix on September 5th, in a *patache*, with twelve sailors and two savages as

[1] Norumbega was the name applied at that time to a vast tract of country whose limits were nearly unknown. There was a river and a cape called Norumbega. The river is now the Penobscot, and the cape is the southern extremity of the Acadian peninsula.

EXPLORATIONS OF 1604

guides. On the first day he covered twenty-five leagues and discovered many islands, reefs and rocks. To another island, four or five leagues in length, he gave the name of Ile des Monts Déserts,[1] which name has been preserved. On the following day Champlain met some hunting Indians of the Etchemin tribe, proceeding from the Pentagouet River to Mount Desert Island. "I think this river," says Champlain, "is that which several pilots and historians call Norumbega, and which most have described as large and extensive, with very many islands, its mouth being in latitude 43°, 43′, 30″. . . . It is related also that there is a large, thickly-settled town of savages, who are adroit and skilful, and who have cotton yarn. I am confident that most of those who mention it have not seen it, and speak of it because they have heard persons say so, who know no more about it than they themselves. . . . But that any one has ever entered it there is no evidence, for then they would have described it in another manner, in order to relieve the minds of many of this doubt."

Champlain's description is written from personal

[1] The Indians called this island *Pemetig*, which means *the island which is ahead*. The French settled here in 1613, and founded St. Sauveur on the north-eastern coast, in a splendid harbour which is to-day known as Bar Harbour. The remains of many of the French who were killed during the contest with the English, were interred at Point Fernald. At the point nearest the mainland there is a bridge of seven hundred feet in length, which communicates with the town of Trenton.

CHAMPLAIN

knowledge, because he had seen the Pentagouet River.[1] The country which it passes through is agreeable, but there was no town or village, and no appearance of either, with the exception of a few deserted cabins of the Souriquois or Micmacs.

Here Champlain met two Souriquois chiefs, Bessabé and Cabahis, and succeeded in making them understand that he had been sent by de Monts to visit their country, and to assure them of the friendship of the French for the Souriquois. Champlain continued his journey southwards, and two days later he again met Cabahis, of whom he asked particulars as to the source of the river Norumbega. The chief replied " that past the falls already mentioned, and after passing some further distance up the river, it widens into a lake, by way of which the Indians pass to the river Ste. Croix, by going some distance overland and then entering the river Etchemin. Another river also enters the lake, along which they proceed for some days until they gain another lake and pass through it. Reaching the end of it they again make a land journey of some distance until they reach another small river, the mouth of which is within a league of Quebec." This little river is the Chaudière, which the Indians follow to reach Quebec. On

[1] Champlain called the river *Peimtegoüet*. This word means *the place of a river where rapids exist*. The English have given their preference to the word *Penobscot*, which comes from the Indian *Penaouasket*, *the place where the earth is covered with stones*.

EXPLORATIONS OF 1605

September 20th Champlain observed the mountains of Bedabedec, and after having proceeded for ten or twelve leagues further he decided to return to Ste. Croix and wait until the following year to continue his explorations. His opinion was that the region he had explored was quite as unfavourable for a settlement as Ste. Croix.

On June 18th, 1605, de Monts, at the head of an expedition consisting of Champlain, some gentlemen, twelve sailors and an Indian guide named Panounias and his wife, set out from the island of Ste. Croix to explore the country of the Almouchiquois, and reached the Pentagouet River in twelve days. On July 1st they made about twenty leagues between Bedabedec Point and the Kennebec River, at the mouth of which is an island which they named *La Tortue* (Segelen Island).

Continuing their journey towards the south they observed some large mountains, the abode of an Indian chief named Aneda. "I was satisfied from the name," says Champlain, "that he was one of his tribe that had discovered the plant called *aneda*, which Jacques Cartier said was so powerful against the malady called scurvy, which harassed his company as well as our own when they wintered in Canada. The savages have no knowledge at all of this plant, and are not aware of its existence, although the above mentioned savage has the same name." This supposition was unfounded, because if this Indian had been of the same origin as the

CHAMPLAIN

aborigines who acquainted Jacques Cartier with the virtue of the *aneda* plant in cases of scruvy, he would have understood the meaning of the word. *Aneda* is the Iroquois word for the spruce tree, but there is no evidence to prove that Champlain was ever aware that it was a specific. Had he known of its efficacy he would have certainly employed it.

At Chouacoet de Monts and Champlain received visits from many Indians, differing entirely from either the Etchemins or the Souriquois. They found the soil tilled and cultivated, and the corn in the gardens was about two feet in height. Beans, pumpkins and squash were also in flower. The place was very pleasant and agreeable at the time, but Champlain believed the weather was very severe in the winter.

The party proceeded still further south, in sight of the Cap aux Iles (Cape Porpoise), and on July 17th, 1605, they came to anchor at Cape St. Louis[1] (Brant Point), where an Indian chief named Honabetha paid them a visit. To a small river which they found in the vicinity they gave the name of Gua, in honour of de Monts. The expedition passed the night of the 18th in a small bay called Plymouth Harbour. On the 19th they observed the cape of a large bay, which they distinguished by the title of Ste. Suzanne du Cap Blanc (Cape Cod), and on

---

[1] The Pilgrim Fathers, the founders of New England, landed near this place, which they named Plymouth, to preserve the name of the English city from which they had sailed.

SETTLEMENT OF PORT ROYAL

July 20th they entered a spacious harbour, which proved to be very dangerous on account of shoals and banks; they therefore named it Mallebarre.

Five weeks had now elapsed since the expedition had left Ste. Croix, and no incident of importance had occurred. They had met many tribes of Indians, and on each occasion their intercourse was harmonious. It is true that they had not traversed more than three degrees of latitude, but, although their progress was slow, their time was well spent. De Monts was satisfied that it would be easier to colonize Acadia than this American coast, and Champlain was still convinced that Port Royal was the most favourable spot, unless de Monts preferred Quebec.

The expedition returned to Ste. Croix in nine days, arriving there on August 3rd. Here they found a vessel from France, under the command of Captain des Antons, laden with provisions, and many things suitable for winter use. There was now a chance of saving the settlers, although their position was not enviable.

De Monts was determined to try the climate of Port Royal, and to endeavour to establish a settlement there. Two barques were fitted out and laden with the frame work of the buildings at Ste. Croix. Champlain and Pont-Gravé had set out before to select a favourable site around the bay, well sheltered from the north-west wind. They chose a place opposite an island at the mouth of the river de

CHAMPLAIN

l'Equille, as being the most suitable. Every one was soon busily engaged in clearing the ground and in erecting houses. The plan of the settlement, says Champlain, was ten fathoms long and eight fathoms wide, making the distance around thirty-six fathoms. On the eastern side was a storehouse occupying the width of it, with a very fine cellar, from five to six feet deep. On the northern side were the quarters of Sieur de Monts, comfortably finished. On the west side were the dwellings of the workmen. At the corner of the western side was a platform, upon which four cannon were placed, and at the eastern corner a palisade was constructed in the shape of a platform. There was nothing pretentious or elegant about these buildings, but they were solid and useful.

The installation of the new settlement being now complete, de Monts returned to France, leaving Pont-Gravé in command. During the absence of de Monts, Champlain determined to pursue his discoveries along the American coast, and in this design he was favoured by de Monts, as the latter had not altogether abandoned his idea of settling in Florida. The season, however, was too far advanced, and Champlain therefore stopped at the river St. John to meet Secoudon, with whom he agreed to set out in search of the famous copper mine. They were accompanied by a miner named Jacques, and a Slavonian very skilful in discovering minerals. He found some pieces of copper and what

EXPLORATIONS OF 1606

appeared to be a mine, but it was too difficult to work. Champlain accordingly returned to Port Royal, where several of the men were suffering from scurvy. Out of forty-five, twelve died during the winter. The surgeon from Honfleur, named Deschamps, performed an autopsy on some of the bodies, and found them affected in the same manner as those who had died at Ste. Croix. Snow did not fall until December 20th, and the winter was not so severe as the previous one.

On March 16th, 1606, Champlain resumed his explorations, and travelled eighteen leagues on that day. He anchored at an island to the south of Manan. During the night his barque ran ashore and sustained injuries which it required four days to repair. Champlain then proceeded to Port aux Coquilles, seven or eight leagues distant, where he remained until the twenty-ninth. Pont-Gravé, however, desired him to return to Port Royal, being anxious to obtain news of his companions whom he had left sick. Owing to indisposition, Champlain was obliged to delay his departure until April 8th.

Champlain and Pont-Gravé intended to return to France during the summer of 1606. Seeing that the vessels promised by de Monts had not arrived, they set out from Port Royal to Cape Breton or Gaspé, in search of a vessel to cross the Atlantic, but when they were approaching Canseau, they met Ralleau, the secretary of de Monts, who informed them that a vessel had been despatched

CHAMPLAIN

under the command of Poutrincourt, with fifty settlers for the country They, therefore, returned to Port Royal, where they found Poutrincourt, who as lieutenant-general of de Monts intended to remain at Port Royal during the year.

On September 5th, Champlain left Port Royal on a voyage of discovery. Poutrincourt joined the expedition, and they took with them a physician, the carpenter Champdoré, and Robert Gravé, the son of François. This last voyage, undertaken to please de Monts, did not result in anything remarkable. They first paid a visit to Ste. Croix, where everything remained unchanged, although the gardens were flourishing. From Ste. Croix the expedition drifted southwards, and Champlain pointed out the same bays, harbours, capes and mountains that he had observed before. Secoudon, chief of the Etchemins, and Messamouet, captain of the Micmacs, joined the party, and proceeded with them as far as Chouacouet, where they intended to form an alliance with Olmechin and Marchin, two Indian chiefs of this country.

On October 2nd, 1606, the expedition reached Mallebarre, and for a few days they anchored in a bay near Cape Batturier, which they named Port Fortuné (Stage Harbour). Five or six hundred savages were found at this place. "It would be an excellent place," says Champlain, "to erect buildings, and lay the foundation of a state, if the harbour was somewhat deeper and the entrance

RETURN TO PORT ROYAL

safer." Poutrincourt stopped here for some days, and in the meantime visited all the surrounding country, from which he returned much pleased.

According to a custom peculiar to the French since the days of Jacques Cartier, de Monts had planted a large cross at the entrance of the Kennebec River, and also at Mallebarre. Poutrincourt did the same at Port Fortuné. The Indians seemed annoyed at this ceremony, which they evidently considered as an encroachment upon their rights as proprietors. They exhibited symptoms of discontent, and during the night killed four Frenchmen who had imprudently stayed ashore. They were buried near the cross. This the Indians immediately threw down, but Poutrincourt ordered it to be restored to its former position.

On three different occasions the party attempted to pursue their discoveries southwards, but they were prevented each time by a contrary wind. They therefore resolved to return to Port Royal, which was rendered imperative by both the approach of winter and the scarcity of provisions. The result of the voyage was not altogether satisfactory. Champlain had reached only a third of a degree further south than on the former occasion, but he had not discovered anything of importance.

On their return to Port Royal, the voyagers were received with great ceremony. Lescarbot, a Parisian lawyer, who had arrived some time before, and

CHAMPLAIN

some other Frenchmen, went to meet them and conducted them to the fort, which had been decorated with evergreens and inscriptions. On the principal door they had placed the arms of France, surrounded with laurel crowns, and the king's motto: *Duo protegit unus*. Beneath the arms of de Monts was placed this inscription: *Dabit Deus his quoque finem*. The arms of Poutrincourt were wreathed with crowns of leaves, with his motto: *Invia virtuti nulla est via*. Lescarbot had composed a short drama for the occasion, entitled, *Le Théatre de Neptune*.

The winter of 1606-07 was not very severe. The settlers lived happily in spite of the scurvy, from which some of them died. Hunting afforded them the means of providing a great variety of dishes, such as geese, ducks, bears, beavers, partridges, reindeer, bustards, etc. They also organized a society devoted to good cheer called, *Ordre du Bon Temps*, the by-laws of which were definite, and were fixed by Champlain himself. The Indians of the vicinity who were friendly towards the French colony were in need of food, so that each day loaves of bread were distributed amongst them. Their *sagamo*, named Membertou, was admitted as a guest to the table of Poutrincourt. This famous Souriquois, who was very old at that time—probably a hundred years, though he had not a single white hair—pretended to have known Jacques Cartier at the time of his first voyage, and claimed

LESCARBOT

that in 1534 he was married, and the father of a young family.

Lescarbot, who was an able man and a good historian, records the particulars above related, besides many other interesting facts concerning Port Royal which appear to have escaped Champlain's observation. Lescarbot was an active spirit in the life of the first French colony in Acadia. He encouraged his companions to cultivate their land, and he worked himself in the gardens, sowing wheat, oats, beans, pease, and herbs, which he tended with care. He was also liked by the Indians, and he would have rejoiced to see them converted to Christianity. Lescarbot was a poet and a preacher, and had also a good knowledge of the arts and of medicine. Charlevoix says: "He daily invented something new for the public good. And there was never a stronger proof of what a new settlement might derive from a mind cultivated by study, and induced by patriotism to use its knowledge and reflections. We are indebted to this advocate for the best memoirs of what passed before his eyes, and for a history of French Florida. We there behold an exact and judicious writer, a man with views of his own, and who would have been as capable of founding a colony as of writing its history."

With the departure of Lescarbot and Champlain the best page of the history of Port Royal is closed. The two men left Canso on September 3rd, 1607,

CHAMPLAIN

on board the *Jonas*, commanded by Nicholas Martin. They stopped at Roscoff in Basse-Bretagne, and the vessel arrived at St. Malo in the early days of October.

Poutrincourt, his son Biencourt, and Lescarbot made a pilgrimage to Mont St. Michel, and Champlain went to Brouage, his native country, having sojourned in America for three years and five months. During that period he had been as continuously active in exploration as the climate allowed, keeping careful record of his travels and making maps and charts for the volume which was to be published half a dozen years later.[1] Even on the return journey he spent the three weeks, after his departure from Port Royal on August 11th, in detailed examination of the coast from there to Canso, where he took ship for France.

[1] Champlain's account of his years in Acadia is contained in Book I of *Les Voyages du Sieur de Champlain*, Paris, 1613. English versions are to be found in *The Works of Samuel de Champlain* (Champlain Society), ed. Biggar, vol. i, and in W. L. Grant's edition of the *Voyages 1604-1618*, Scribners, New York, 1907.

CHAPTER III

THE FOUNDING OF QUEBEC

AFTER his return to France, as before described, Champlain had an interview with de Monts, and laid before him the journal which he had prepared of his explorations in America, together with plans of the ports and coasts which he had minutely examined during his visits. Champlain proposed to de Monts to continue his explorations, and advanced some reasons for prosecuting an enterprise upon which a large sum had been already expended, and which he was persuaded would ultimately afford the means of repairing their fortunes. De Monts, owing to the failure of his own efforts as a colonizer, was not at first inclined to listen to Champlain's proposals, but he was finally convinced of the wisdom of his suggestions, and appointed him lieutenant of an expedition to Quebec for the purpose of trading with the Indians. The expedition was to return to France during the same year. De Monts obtained another commission from the king, dated at Paris, January 9th, 1608, which gave him the monopoly of the fur trade in the lands, ports and rivers of Canada for a period of one year. Two vessels were equipped for this expedition, the *Don de Dieu*, captain Henry Couillard, and the

CHAMPLAIN

Lévrier, captain Nicholas Marion. Champlain was given the command of the former vessel, and Pont-Gravé was in command of the latter. The *Lévrier* sailed from France on April 5th, and the *Don de Dieu* eight days later. The two vessels proceeded directly to Tadousac, without calling at Percé, according to the usual custom.

On the arrival of the *Don de Dieu* at Tadousac, Champlain found that Pont-Gravé had been attacked by Captain Darache, a Basque, who continued to trade for furs with the Indians in spite of the king's commands. Darache had brought all his guns to bear upon the *Lévrier*, and Pont-Gravé being unable to defend himself, had offered no resistance, whereupon Darache's crew had boarded the vessel and carried off the cannon and arms, at the same time intimating that they would continue to trade as they pleased. The arrival of Champlain, however, altered the situation, and Darache was compelled to sign an agreement by which he pledged himself not to molest Pont-Gravé, or to do anything prejudicial to the interest of the king or of de Monts. It was also agreed that all differences should be settled by the authorities in France. After this agreement was effected through Champlain's intervention, the carpenters of the expedition fitted out a small barque to convey to Quebec all the articles necessary for the use of the future settlement.

In the meantime Champlain visited the river Saguenay, where he met some Indians from whom

QUEBEC, 1608

he gathered information concerning Lake St. John and its tributaries. The information did not differ greatly from that which he had obtained in the year 1603. Champlain set out from Tadousac on the last day of June and arrived at Quebec on July 3rd, "Where I searched," he says, "for a place suitable for our settlement, but I could find none more convenient or better situated than the point of Quebec, so called by the savages, which was covered with nut trees."

Champlain was accompanied by thirty men, amongst whom may be named Nicholas Marsolet, Étienne Brûlé, Bonnerme, a doctor, Jean Duval, Antoine Natel and La Taille. These names are specially recorded. Champlain immediately employed some workmen to fell trees in order to commence the construction of an *Habitation*. One party was engaged in sawing timber, another in digging a cellar and some ditches, while another party was sent to Tadousac with a barque to obtain supplies which had been retained in the ships. Such was the beginning of Champlain's city. Nothing great, it will be admitted, for a settlement which its founder hoped before long would become the great warehouse of New France.

Until this date the merchants had traded with the Indians only in those places where they could easily be met, and even Chauvin, who was mentioned in a previous chapter, had not gone further than Tadousac. Neither Three Rivers, nor the

CHAMPLAIN

islands of Sorel at the entrance of the Iroquois River, now called the Richelieu River, were known to French navigators at this period, and although these places were easily accessible to the aborigines, they were not so available as Quebec.

Champlain well understood the advantages of founding his city on a spot naturally fortified and where he could readily defend himself against the attack of an enemy, whose approach he expected sooner or later. The first foes, however, whom Champlain had to encounter were not the Indians, but his own countrymen, members of his crew who under various pretexts sought to kill their chief and give the command of the settlement to the Basques. Jean Duval, the king's locksmith, was the leader of this conspiracy against Champlain, and associated with him were four vicious sailors to whom he promised a part of the reward which had been offered for this treason. The conspirators agreed to preserve secrecy, and fixed the night of the fourth day for the assassination of their chief.

On the day upon which the plot was to be put into execution, Captain Le Testu[1] arrived from Tadousac in command of a vessel laden with provisions, utensils, etc. After the vessel was unloaded, one of the conspirators, a locksmith named

[1] Le Testu's Christian name was Guillaume. His first voyage to Newfoundland was made in 1601. He came to Quebec in 1608, 1610, 1611, 1612, 1613, 1614, and 1616. He was successively captain of the *Fleur de Lys*, the *Trinité*, and the *Nativité*. He was very circumspect in his dealings.

THE CONSPIRACY FRUSTRATED

Natel, approached the captain and acquainted him with the details of the plot. Champlain also listened to the man's account and promised to observe secrecy, although he took precautions to frustrate the scheme by inviting the leader and the four conspirators to an entertainment on board Captain Le Testu's barque.

The men accepted the invitation, and as soon as they were on board they were seized and held in custody until the following day. The deposition of each man was then taken by Champlain in the presence of the pilot and sailors, and set down in writing, after which the "worthies" were sent to Tadousac, where Champlain requested Pont-Gravé to guard them for a time. Some days after the men were returned to Quebec, where they were placed on trial for attempted murder.

The jury was composed of Champlain, Pont-Gravé, Le Testu, Bonnerme, the mate and the second mate, and some sailors. The verdict was unanimous. Duval was condemned to death on the spot as the instigator of the plot, and the others were also sentenced to death, but their sentence was to be carried out in France. Duval was strangled at Quebec, and his head was placed on a pike which was set up in the most conspicuous part of the fort. This was the second example of capital punishment in New France. The first case recorded was at Charlesbourg Royal, or Cap-Rouge, near Quebec, in the winter of 1542-3, when Michel

CHAMPLAIN

Gaillon, one of Roberval's companions, was put to death.

Champlain was invested with executive, legislative and judiciary powers, but the founder of Quebec never abused the authority intrusted to him. From this time every one fulfilled his duty day by day, and Champlain was able to continue his work in peace.

The habitation was composed of three buildings of two stories, each one of three fathoms long and two and a half wide. The storehouse was six fathoms long and three wide, with a cellar six feet deep. There was a gallery around the buildings, at the second story. There were also ditches fifteen feet wide and six deep. On the outer side of the ditches Champlain constructed several spurs, which enclosed a part of the dwelling, at the point where he placed a cannon. Before the habitation there was a square four fathoms wide and six or seven long, looking out upon the river bank. Surrounding the habitation were very good gardens, and an open space on the north side, some hundred and twenty paces long and fifty or sixty wide.

During the first weeks after his installation, Champlain made an investigation of the vicinity. "Near Quebec," he says, "there is a little river coming from a lake in the interior, distant six or seven leagues from our settlement. I am of opinion that this river, which is north a quarter north-west from our settlement, is the place where Jacques

JACQUES CARTIER'S DWELLING

Cartier wintered, since there are still, a league up the river, remains of what seems to have been a chimney, the foundation of which has been found, and indications of there having been ditches surrounding their dwelling, which was small. We found also, large pieces of hewn, worm-eaten timber, and some three or four cannon balls. All these things show clearly that there was a settlement there founded by Christians; and what leads me to say and believe that it was that of Jacques Cartier is the fact that there is no evidence whatever that any one wintered and built a house in these places except Jacques Cartier at the time of his discoveries."

This "little river coming from a lake in the interior," is evidently the river St. Charles, called Ste. Croix by Cartier. Champlain's conjectures about the place where Jacques Cartier wintered, are certainly correct. It was near this spot also that the Jesuits erected their convent of Notre Dame des Anges in 1626, namely, at two hundred feet from the shore, where the river Lairet joins the St. Charles.

Pont-Gravé sailed for France on September 18th, 1608, leaving Champlain with twenty-seven men, and provisions for the approaching winter at Quebec. The carpenters, sawyers, and other workmen were employed in clearing up the place and in preparing gardens.

Many Indians were encamped in the vicinity,

CHAMPLAIN

who proved troublesome neighbours, as they were constantly visiting the habitation, either to beg food for their families or to express their fear of invisible enemies. Champlain readily understood the character of these people, but he was too charitable to refuse them assistance in their need; besides he believed that they might easily be taught how to live and how to cultivate the soil. It was a difficult task, however, to induce the Indians to settle in any particular place. For generations they had led a wandering life, subsisting on the products of their hunting and fishing. This wild freedom was as necessary to their existence as the open air, and all attempts to make them follow the habits of civilized races seemed to tend towards their deterioration.

The early days of the French settlement at Quebec were distinguished by nothing remarkable. During the first winter scurvy and dysentery claimed many victims. Natel, the locksmith, died towards the end of November, and some time after Bonnerme, the doctor, was attacked and succumbed. Eighteen others also suffered from scurvy of whom ten died, and there were five deaths from dysentery, so that by the spring there were only eight men living, and Champlain himself was seriously indisposed. This was the third time that the founder of Quebec had had to experience the effects of this terrible disease, and although he was beginning to understand its causes, he was still unaware of a

THE IROQUOIS TERRITORY

specific. "I am confident," he says, "that, with good bread and fresh meat, a person would not be liable to it."

Many trials had been experienced by the settlers during their first winter of 1608-09, and they welcomed the return of spring. Des Marets[1] arrived at Quebec at this time, with tidings that Pont-Gravé, his father-in-law, had arrived at Tadousac on May 28th. Champlain at once repaired to Tadousac, where he received a letter from de Monts requesting him to return to France to acquaint him with the progress which he had made in the colony, and with the result of his explorations. Champlain returned to Quebec, and immediately fitted out an expedition to visit the country of the Iroquois, in the company of a party of Montagnais.

The Montagnais were anxious to carry on war against their ancient enemies, and although the wars had no attraction for Champlain, he hoped to be able to further his discoveries during the journey. Taking with him the twenty men placed at his disposal by Pont-Gravé, Champlain sailed from Quebec on June 18th, 1609. The command of the

[1] Champlain often speaks of this man. His true name was Claude Godet, Sieur des Marets. His father, Cléophas Godet, a lawyer, had three sons, Claude, Jean and Jessé. Jean was Sieur du Parc, and Jessé parish priest of Chambois in 1634. Both Claude and Jean came to Canada. Claude des Marets was married, in 1615, to Jeanne Gravé, only daughter of François Gravé, Sieur du Pont. He died about the year 1626, leaving one child named François, who came to New France with his grandfather, and was present at the capitulation of Quebec in 1629.

CHAMPLAIN

habitation was given to Pont-Gravé in the meantime. The expedition proceeded towards the island of St. Eloi, near the shores of which two or three hundred savages were encamped in tents. They proved to be Hurons and Algonquins who were on their way to Quebec to join Champlain's expedition to the territory of the Iroquois. Their chiefs were named Iroquet and Ochateguin, and Champlain explained to them the object of his voyage. The next day the two chiefs paid a visit to Champlain and remained silent for some time, meditating and smoking. After some reflection the chiefs began to harangue their companions on the banks of the river. They spoke for a long time in loud tones, and the substance of their remarks has been summed up in these words:—

"Ten moons ago Champlain had declared that he desired to assist them against their enemies, with whom they had been for a long time at warfare, on account of many cruel acts committed by them against their tribe, under colour of friendship. Having ever since longed for vengeance, they had solicited all the savages whom they had seen on the banks of the river to come and make an alliance. They had no children with them but men versed in war and full of courage, and well acquainted with the country and the rivers of the land of the Iroquois. They wanted to go to Quebec in order that they might see the French houses, but after three days they would return to engage in the war. As a

THE INDIAN ALLIANCE

token of firm friendship and joy, Champlain should have muskets and arquebuses fired."

Champlain replied that he was glad to be able to fulfil his promise to them; he had no other purpose than to assist them in their wars; he had not come as a trader, but only with arms to fight. His word was given, and it was his desire that it should be kept. Thus was the alliance ratified which had been made in 1603 between the French and the Hurons, Algonquins and Montagnais, and the alliance was never broken.

Some historians have reproached Champlain for his intervention in the wars between the Indians of Canada, and have suggested that it would have been wiser to have preserved a strict neutrality, instead of taking up arms against the redoubtable and valiant Iroquois. In order to explain Champlain's actions, it is necessary to consider the relations of the French towards the other tribes. Many years before the period of which we are writing, certain French captains traded with the Montagnais Indians of Tadousac. These Indians were on friendly terms with the Hurons, the Algonquins Supérieurs of the Ottawa river, and the Souriquois of Acadia, and were united in their desire to subdue the terrible Iroquois. As the Iroquois did not trade with the French, Champlain had no relations with them of a business character, and therefore he was not bound towards them in the same manner as he was towards the Hurons and others.

CHAMPLAIN

The Iroquois at first resided at Montreal and Three Rivers, while their neighbours, the Algonquins, were scattered along the shores of the Ottawa River, Lake Nipissing and French River. The Algonquins, who were brave and very numerous, succeeded in driving the Iroquois back to Lake Erie, and afterwards to Lake Ontario, near Lake Champlain. Here the Iroquois were distributed in five tribes, forming a great confederation. (1.) The Tsonnontouans or Senecas. (2.) The Goyogouins or Cayugas. (3.) The Onontagues or Onondagas. (4.) The Onneyouts or Oneidas. (5.) The Agniers or Mohawks. The Tsonnontouans were the most numerous, but the Agniers were the bravest and wildest.

The Iroquois or confederate tribes had by constant warfare become the greatest warriors of New France, nor is this fact surprising when we consider that they had waged successful warfare, extending over a long period, against the vast coalition of Hurons, Algonquins, Montagnais and Micmacs scattered from Lake Huron to Acadia.

Anadabijou, chief of the Montagnais, made a long speech, telling his men that they ought to feel proud of the friendship of the king of France and of his people, upon whom they could rely for assistance in their wars. It was from that date that the alliance between the Indians and the French commenced, and, as Champlain was obliged to live in the neighbourhood of the Montagnais and Al-

THE ALLIANCE SEALED

gonquins, the only course open to him, if he desired to live in peace, was to fulfil his promise made to them.

In this year, 1609, Anadabijou reminded Champlain of the agreement made six years before. " Ten moons ago," he says, "the son of Iroquet had seen you. You gave him a good reception, and promised with Pont-Gravé to assist us against our enemies." To this Champlain replied, " My only desire is to fulfil what I promised then." Thus was sealed this solemn agreement.

If Champlain had refused to make an alliance with these Indians, they would have been a constant source of trouble, for although they were less ferocious than the Iroquois, they were still barbarians. Champlain and his few men could never have established a settlement at Quebec if they had been forced to encounter the hostility of the neighbouring Indians, for the whole of his work could have been overthrown by them in a single day.

The country of the Iroquois, on the contrary, was situated at a great distance, and consequently he had not so much to fear from them. It was Champlain's desire, however, to make a treaty with the Iroquois as well, for they were at this time even, and long after remained, the terror of North America. But war seemed necessary to the existence of the Iroquois, and Champlain, notwithstanding the exercise of his diplomacy, found it impossible to pacify these restless people.

CHAMPLAIN

It is true that the people of New Holland had been able to maintain a neutral stand towards the Iroquois, and Champlain has been blamed for not following this example. It must be borne in mind, however, that the Dutch were powerful and numerous, and it was to their interest to live in harmony with their immediate neighbours, the Iroquois. The Dutch had also different intentions towards the Indians. They came to America simply to trade, and to establish themselves and live quietly along the shores of the Hudson River, while Champlain's idea was to civilize the Indians and bring them under the influence of the Catholic missionaries

Champlain and the allied Indians left Quebec on June 28th, 1609. Des Marets, La Routte, a pilot, and nine men accompanied the expedition. On their voyage they passed certain rivers to which Champlain gave the following names, Ste. Suzanne (River du Loup), du Pont (Nicolet), de Gênes (Yamaska), and the Three Rivers.[1] The party stopped at the entrance of the Iroquois River. Continuing their journey southwards, they arrived at the Chambly Rapids. "No Christians had been in this place before us," says Champlain. Seeing no prospect of being able to cross the rapids alone, Champlain enbarked with the Indians in their canoes, taking

---

[1] This is the river *de Fouez* of Jacques Cartier, and the *Metaberoutin* of the Indians, and now the river St. Maurice, to which has been given by Champlain the name of Three Rivers, because two islands divide it into three branches at its entrance; these branches are called *Les Chenaux*, or the narrow channels.

DEFEAT OF THE IROQUOIS

only two men with him. Champlain's army, comprising sixty men, then proceeded slowly towards Lake Champlain, down which they sailed towards Lake St. Sacrament (Lake George). On July 29th they encountered the Iroquois, who had come to fight, at the extremity of Lake Champlain, on the western bank. The entire night was spent by each army in dancing and singing, and in bandying words. At daybreak Champlain's men stood to arms. The Iroquois were composed of about two hundred men, stout and rugged in appearance, with their three chiefs at their head, who could be distinguished by their large plumes. The allies opened their ranks and called upon Champlain to go to the front. The arrows were beginning to fly on both sides when Champlain discharged his musket, which was loaded with four balls, and killed two of the chiefs and mortally wounded the third. This unexpected blow caused great alarm among the Iroquois, who lost courage, abandoned their camp and took to flight, seeking shelter in the woods. Fifteen or sixteen men of Champlain's party were wounded, but the enemy had many wounded, and ten or twelve were taken prisoners.

This victory did not entail much hardship on the part of the French. Champlain and his two companions did more to rout the Iroquois than the sixty allies with their shower of arrows. The result of this day's proceedings was highly satisfactory to the Indians, who gathered up the arms and provi-

CHAMPLAIN

sions left behind by the Iroquois, and feasted sumptuously amidst dancing and singing. "The spot where this attack took place," says Champlain, "is in the latitude of 43° and some minutes, and the lake is called Champlain." This place is now called Ticonderoga, or the Cheondoroga of the Indians.

Champlain returned to Quebec with the Montagnais, and a few days after he set out for Tadousac to see whether Pont-Gravé had arrived from Gaspé. He met Pont-Gravé on the morrow, and they both decided to sail for France, and to leave Quebec in the meantime under the command of Pierre de Chauvin,[1] pending the decision of de Monts as to the future of the colony. Both visited Quebec in order to invest Chauvin with authority, and after leaving him everything necessary for the use of the settlement, and placing fifteen men under his command, the two commanders left Quebec on September 1st, 1609, and sailed from Tadousac for France on the fifth day of the same month.

Champlain had sojourned in New France since the beginning of July, 1608, and during that interval he had made good use of his time. He had chosen the most suitable place for a habitation which was destined to become the metropolis of the

[1] Pierre de Chauvin, Sieur de la Pierre, called Captain Pierre by Champlain, was born at Dieppe, but after the death of his relative, Pierre de Chauvin, Sieur de Tontuit, he resided at Honfleur. There were many families of Chauvin in Normandy during the seventeenth century, notably the Chauvins, Sieurs de Tontuit, and the Chauvins, Sieurs de la Pierre.

SATISFACTORY RESULTS

French colony; he had constructed a fort and a storehouse, and he had also explored a very important tract of country. Champlain had also visited a part of the river Saguenay; he had made himself acquainted with the vicinity of Quebec, and with the rivers, streams and tributaries of the St. Lawrence and Ste. Croix. For the second time he had seen the river St. Lawrence as far as the Iroquois River over which he had sailed as far as Lake Champlain, whence it receives its waters. Besides his achievements in exploration Champlain had cemented friendly relations with the Montagnais, Algonquins and Hurons; he had renewed his acquaintance with Anadabijou and formed an alliance with Iroquet and Ochateguin, three of the most powerful chiefs of these tribes. He was also well versed in their methods of warfare and had studied their manners and customs and their treatment of their prisoners, so that when he returned to France he was in a position to give de Monts a great deal of valuable information, both as regards the inhabitants and the best means of promoting trade with them.

On his arrival in France Champlain proceeded at once to Fontainebleau, where he met King Henry IV and de Monts. He had an audience with the king and gave His Majesty a satisfactory account of his proceedings. He also presented to the king a girdle made of porcupine quills, two little birds of carnation colour, and the head of a fish caught in

CHAMPLAIN

Lake Champlain, which had a very long snout, and two or three rows of very sharp teeth.

To de Monts the visit of Champlain was of great importance, because the fate of Quebec was bound up with him. After hearing Champlain's narrative of his voyages in New France, de Monts decided to visit Rouen in order to consult Collier and Legendre, his associates. After deliberation they resolved to continue their efforts to colonize New France and to further explore the great river St. Lawrence. In order to realize means for defraying the expenses of the expedition, Pont-Gravé was authorized to engage in any traffic that would help to accomplish this end. In the meantime Lucas Legendre was ordered to purchase merchandise for the expedition, to see to the repairs of the vessels, and to obtain crews. After these details had been arranged de Monts and Champlain returned to Paris to settle the more important questions.

De Monts' commission, which had been issued for one year, had expired, but he hoped that it would be renewed. His requests, which appeared just and reasonable, were, however, refused, owing to protests on the part of merchants of Brittany and Normandy, who claimed that this monopoly was ruinous to their commerce. Finally de Monts appealed to his former partners, who decided to furnish two vessels, at their own expense, with supplies and stores necessary for the settlement. Pont-Gravé was given the command of a fur-trad-

EXPEDITION OF 1610

ing vessel, and the other was laden with provisions and stores necessary for the use of the settlers. Champlain was informed that his services were dispensed with, but not believing that this news could be true, he saw de Monts and asked him frankly whether such was the case. De Monts told him that he could accompany the expedition, if he chose to do so. Champlain therefore set out from Paris on the last day of February, 1610, and proceeded to Rouen, where he remained for two days, and then left for Honfleur, to meet Pont-Gravé and Legendre, who informed him that the vessels were ready to sail.

CHAPTER IV

CHAMPLAIN'S VOYAGES OF 1610, 1611, 1613

CHAMPLAIN embarked at Honfleur with eleven artisans for Quebec, on March 7th, 1610. The rough weather experienced during the first days of the voyage rendered it necessary for the vessel to run into Portland, on the English coast, and later to seek refuge in the lee of the Isle of Wight. At this time Champlain was taken suddenly ill, and was obliged to return by boat to Havre de Grâce to undergo medical treatment. A month after he rejoined his former vessel, which in the meantime had returned to Honfleur to take in ballast. Champlain had now somewhat recovered, although he was still weak and ill.

The vessel left Honfleur on April 8th, and reached Tadousac on the 26th of the same month, which was one of the shortest passages ever made up to that time. "There were vessels," says Champlain, "which had arrived on the 18th of the month, a thing which had not been seen for more than sixty years, as the old mariners said who sail regularly to this country." This remark proves that for more than half a century French fishermen and navigators had been accustomed to proceed as far as Tadousac. A Basque, named Lavalette, who had been accustomed to fish on the Acadian coast from about the year 1565, also confirms the statement.

On his arrival at Tadousac, Champlain ascertained from a young nobleman, named du Parc,[1] who had wintered with Chauvin at Quebec, that all the settlers were in good health, and that only a few of them had been slightly ill. They had been able to procure fresh meat during the whole season, and consequently scurvy had not made its appearance. "By avoiding salt food and using fresh meat, the health is as good here as in France."

The Indians had been waiting from day to day for the return of Champlain, for they wished him to accompany them to war. He therefore went ashore to assure them that he would fulfil his promise under the conditions made, namely, that upon his return they would point out to him the three rivers, and the lake which they had described as resembling a sea, the end of which could not be seen, and by means of which he could return by way of the Saguenay to Tadousac. The Indians readily promised to do all this, but only in the following year. Champlain had also promised the Hurons and Algonquins that he would assist them in their wars, if they would show him their country, the great lake and the copper mines. "I had accord-

[1] Jean Godet, Sieur du Parc, was a brother of Claude des Marets. He came with his brother to Quebec in 1609, and wintered there. In 1616 he commanded at Quebec. On his return to France, he remained at St. Germain de Clairefeuille, where he died on November 16th, 1652.

A GENERAL RENDEZVOUS

ingly " he said 'two strings to my bow, so that, in case one should break, the other might hold."

On April 28th, 1610, Champlain set out from Tadousac for Quebec, where he found Captain Chauvin and his companions in good health. They had with them an Indian chief named Batiscan, who was so pleased at Champlain's return that he and his comrades showed their appreciation by singing and dancing all night. Champlain entertained them at a banquet, with which they were delighted.

Some days after a party of the Montagnais, numbering about sixty men, made their appearance at Quebec, *en route* for the war. They presented themselves before Champlain, and said: " Here are numerous Basques and Mistigoches (so they named the Normans and Malouins) who say they will go to the war with us. What do you think of it ? Do they speak the truth ?" Champlain answered: " No, I know very well what they really mean; they say this only to get possession of your commodities." The Indians replied : " You have spoken the truth. They are women and want to make war only upon our beavers." Confiding in Champlain's word, the Montagnais went to Three Rivers under the agreement that a general rendezvous should be held there with the French. The Hurons were to await them at the entrance of the Iroquois River.

Champlain started on his journey on June 14th. When he was eight leagues from Quebec he met a canoe bearing an Algonquin and a Montagnais,

CHAMPLAIN

who entreated him to hasten towards Three Rivers, as the Algonquins and Hurons would be at the meeting-place within two days. The Algonquins presented Champlain with a piece of copper a foot long and quite pure, and stated that there were large quantities to be found on the bank of a river, near a great lake. The Indians also stated that they collected the copper in lumps, and after they had melted it, spread it in sheets and smoothed it with stones. Champlain was well pleased to receive this present, although it was of small value.

The Montagnais assembled at Three Rivers, and on June 18th they all set out together. On the following day they arrived at an island situated at the mouth of the river Richelieu, which the Montagnais used to frequent when they wished to avoid the Iroquois.

An alarm was soon given that the Algonquins had fallen in with a band of Iroquois, numbering one hundred, who were strongly barricaded. Each man then took his arms and set out in a canoe towards the enemy. The firing immediately began, and Champlain was wounded by an arrow which pierced his ear and entered his neck. He seized the arrow and withdrew it from the wound. The Iroquois were much astonished at the noise caused by the discharge of the French muskets, and some of them, seeing their companions wounded or dead, threw themselves upon the ground whenever they heard a musket fired. Champlain resolved after

SAVIGNON

a while to force the barricade, sword in hand, which he accomplished without much resistance, and entered the fort. Fifteen prisoners were taken, and the rest were killed either by musket shots, arrows, or the sword. The savages, according to their custom, scalped the dead. The Montagnais and Algonquins had three killed and fifty wounded. On the following day Pont-Gravé and Chauvin did some trading in peltry.

Amongst Champlain's party there was a young lad named Nicholas Marsolet, who desired to accompany the Algonquins in order to learn their language, and he was pleased to learn that after much deliberation the Algonquins had decided to take him, on the condition that Champlain accepted a young Huron as hostage. The Indian boy was named Savignon by the French. Lescarbot writes that he met this youth many times in Paris, and that "he was a big and stout boy."

The French and the allied Indians separated with many promises of friendship. The Indians departed for the fall of the great river of Canada, and the French, with Champlain at their head, proceeded to Quebec. On the return journey they met at Lake St. Peter, Pont-Gravé, who was on his way to Tadousac, to arrange some business connected with headquarters.

Pont-Gravé contemplated passing the winter at Quebec, but in the meantime des Marets arrived from France, much to the delight of every one,

CHAMPLAIN

as his vessel was long overdue. The news which he brought, however, was so serious that both Champlain and Pont-Gravé decided to return to France. The intelligence received was to the effect that M. de St. Luc had expelled the Huguenots from Brouage, that the king had been killed, and that the Duke of Sully and two other noblemen had shared the same fate.

Champlain was much distressed over the condition of affairs in France, and on his departure he left du Parc in command of Quebec, and placed under him sixteen men, "all of whom were enjoined to live soberly, and in the fear of God, and in strict observance of the obedience due to the authority of du Parc." The settlement was left with a plentiful supply of kitchen vegetables, together with a sufficient quantity of Indian corn, wheat, rye and barley. Everything was in good order when Champlain set out from Quebec on August 8th. Five days later Pont-Gravé's vessel sailed from Tadousac for France. On September 27th they arrived at Honfleur, the voyage having lasted one month and a half.

This second voyage of Champlain did not restore de Monts' fortunes. The withdrawal of the exclusive privilege of trading was the signal for a large number of trading vessels to appear in the St. Lawrence. In fact the operations were so great as to render the profits of the company null. The disaster was so complete that Champlain says: "Many will remem-

THOUGHTS OF MARRIAGE

ber for a long time the loss made this year." For all the labour which Champlain had bestowed upon the settlement the result was small, and it was evident that if any French merchant were allowed without restrictions to trade with the Indians, commerce would be ruined, and the development of the settlement would be impossible. During the first years a beaver skin could be exchanged in return for two knives, and now fifteen or twenty were required for the same exchange. Champlain therefore desired to establish some form of rule by which commerce could be restricted, or in other words, whereby he or de Monts, or any one else who would undertake the direction of the affairs of New France, might be protected.

It was during this winter of 1610-11, that Champlain, who was now more than forty years of age, entertained thoughts of marriage. His constant voyages during the past twelve years had probably prevented him from entering into this estate before. It is, perhaps, somewhat surprising that he so suddenly put aside this consideration against the marriage. Did he contemplate residing permanently at Quebec, or did he foresee that circumstances would render his remaining in New France improbable? There is nothing in his narrative which throws any light on this question. Champlain does not mention the name of his wife in any of his writings, but we find later that she accompanied him to Quebec, where she dwelt for four years. The name of Cham-

CHAMPLAIN

plain's wife was Hélène Boullé, the daughter of Nicholas Boullé, secretary of the king's chamber, and of Marguerite Alix of St. Germain l'Auxerrois, Paris. Hélène Boullé was born in 1598, and at the time of her marriage contract she was only twelve years of age. Her parents were Calvinists, and she was brought up in the same faith, but through the lessons and influence of her husband she became a Catholic.

The marriage settlements were executed at Paris on December 27th, 1610, and signed by Choquillet and Arragon, notaries, in the presence of the parents and friends of both parties. Among those who attended on that occasion were Pierre du Gua, friend; Lucas Legendre, of Rouen, friend; Hercule Rouer, merchant of Paris; Marcel Chenu, merchant of Paris; Jehan Roernan, secretary of de Monts, Champlain's friend; François Lesaige, druggist of the king's stables, friend and relative; Jehan Ravenal, Sieur de la Merrois; Pierre Noël, Sieur de Cosigné, friend; Anthoine de Murad, king's councillor and almoner; Anthoine Marye, barber-surgeon, relative and friend; Geneviève Lesaige, wife of Simon Alix, uncle of Hélène Boullé, on the mother's side.

According to the terms of the contract, Nicholas Boullé and his wife pledged themselves, by anticipated payment of the inheritance, to pay six thousand livres cash, the day preceding the marriage. Champlain also agreed to give his future wife the

THE MARRIAGE CEREMONY

benefit of his wealth at his death. Two days after, Nicholas Boullé sent to his son-in-law the sum of four thousand five hundred livres, the balance was to be sent later on.

The betrothal took place in the church of St. Germain l'Auxerrois, on Wednesday, December 29th, 1610. As the young bride was not of marriageable age, she returned to her family to live with them for two years, as agreed by the contract.

Champlain then resumed his colonization work, and had an interview with de Monts, in order to encourage him to continue the enterprise. Although the profits were likely to be small so long as the trade was open, it seemed probable that fur-trading, and developing the resources of the country, might still yield a profit. The expenses of the undertaking were also small: a few barrels of biscuits, of pease and cider would be found sufficient to sustain the fifteen or twenty men who formed the nucleus of the colony. From year to year Champlain hoped to be able to monopolize the fur trade, not for himself, but for the company of de Monts.

The vessels which were equipped for the expedition were ready to sail on March 1st, 1611. The passage was very rough, and when about eight leagues distant from the Great Banks of Newfoundland, the vessels were in great danger through the number of icebergs which were encountered. The cold was so intense that it was found difficult

CHAMPLAIN

to navigate the vessel. While in the vicinity of Newfoundland, they communicated with a French ship, on board of which was Biencourt, son of Poutrincourt, who was bound for Port Royal to meet his father. He had left France three months previously, and had been unable to find his way to the Acadian coast,

After having sighted Gaspé, Champlain arrived at Tadousac on May 13th, where he found all the country covered with snow. The savages were informed of Champlain's arrival by cannon shot, and they soon made their appearance. They stated that three or four trading vessels had arrived within the last eight days, but that their business had been a failure on account of the scarcity of furs.

Champlain proceeded at once to Quebec, where he found everything in good order, and neither du Parc nor his companions had suffered from any sickness. Game had been abundant during the whole winter. Champlain intended to visit Three Rivers, but Batiscan said that he would not be prepared to conduct him there until next year. As he was unable to carry out his designs, Champlain took with him Savignon and one Frenchman, and visited the great fall. He made a careful examination of the country, and says:—

"But in all that I saw I found no place more favourable than a little spot to which barques and shallops can easily ascend with the help of a strong wind, or by taking a winding course, in consequence

THE SITE OF MONTREAL

of the strong current. But above this place, which we named *La Place Royale*, at the distance of a league from Mont Royal, there are a great many little rocks and shoals which are very dangerous. . . . Formerly savages tilled these lands. . . . There is a large number of other fine pastures, where any number of cattle can graze. . . . After a careful examination, we found this place one of the finest on this river. I accordingly gave orders to cut down and clear up the woods in the Place Royale, so as to level it and prepare it for building."

This was the beginning of Montreal, the wealthiest city of Canada.

Champlain constructed a wall four feet thick, three or four feet high, and thirty feet long. This fort was placed on an elevation twelve feet higher than the level of the soil, so that it was safe from inundation. Champlain named the island Ste. Hélène, in honour of his wife, and he found that a strong town could be built there. To-day this island is a favourite resort for the inhabitants of Montreal, and it is an ornament to the harbour of the large city.

On June 13th two hundred Hurons arrived at Sault St. Louis, so called from a young Frenchman named Louis, who was drowned in the rapids a few days before. The Hurons were under the command of Ochateguin, Iroquet and Tregouaroti. The latter was a brother of Savignon, the young Huron whom

CHAMPLAIN

Champlain had taken with him to France. The interview, which lasted some time, was most cordial. The Indians said that they felt somewhat uneasy on seeing so many Frenchmen all so greedy of gain, and that they had desired to see Champlain alone, towards whom they were as kindly disposed as towards their own children.

Champlain questioned them on the sources of the great river, and on their own country. Four of them declared that they had seen a large sea at a great distance from their village. After exchanging their peltry with Champlain's consent, some of the Hurons left to follow the war-path, while others returned to their own country. This interview occurred on June 18th, 1611. Champlain waited at Montreal to meet the Algonquins, who appeared in due course. After cementing the alliance with them, Champlain, on July 18th, set out for Quebec, where he arrived on the nineteenth. Here he found that certain necessary repairs had to be made. He also planted some rose bushes, and caused some oak wood to be placed on board a vessel for shipment to France, as a specimen of the wood of the new colony, which he considered suitable, not only for woodwork of ships, but also for windows and doors.

Champlain sailed from Quebec on July 20th, and arrived at La Rochelle on September 16th. De Monts was at Pons, in Saintonge, at this time, and it was here that he received a visit from Champlain.

END OF DE MONTS' COMPANY

After listening to Champlain's narrative of his proceedings, de Monts decided to proceed to court to arrange matters. He held a conference with his partners at Fontainebleau, but he found that they were unwilling to continue to support the enterprise. He therefore concluded a bargain with them for what remained in the Quebec settlement by the payment of a certain sum of money, and from that date the former company ceased to exist. Only Champlain and Monts retained any faith in the scheme of trade and settlement.

The year 1612 saw a further change. Champlain had sustained a bad fall from a horse in France, and by this, as well as by the affairs of the company, was kept at home all summer. Meanwhile in Canada the trade remained open, and the profits were as small as before. So that after four years of open trade Monts found his fortune sinking instead of rising, and he felt entirely unable to go on under existing conditions. The future of Canada as a settlement depended on what Champlain could achieve. His personal means were small, and far too slender to enable him to support a colony in its infancy. The thought of abandoning the settlement was repugnant to him, not only on account of the years of labour he had bestowed upon it, but also because he felt that there was every chance of success with the aid of rich and powerful men.

At the commencement of his description of his

CHAMPLAIN

fourth voyage to Canada, Champlain enumerates the reasons which induced him to continue his work of discovery: "The desire which I have always had of making new discoveries in New France, for the good, profit and glory of the French name, and at the same time to lead the poor natives to the knowledge of God, has led me to seek more and more for the greater facility of this undertaking, which can only be secured by means of good regulations."

Then he drew up a statement which he handed to President Jeannin, whom he knew to be well disposed.

The president encouraged Champlain but in order that he might not be deceived, he thought it better that Champlain should act under the authority of some man whose influence would be sufficient to protect him against the jealousy of the merchants. Champlain therefore addressed himself through M. de Beaulieu, councillor and almoner in ordinary to the king, to Charles de Bourbon, Comte de Soissons, then governor of Dauphiné and Normandy. He urged upon the count the importance of the undertaking, and explained the best means of regulating it, claiming that the disorders which had hitherto existed threatened to ruin the enterprise, and to bring dishonour to the name of the French.

After having examined the map of the country, and studied the details of the scheme, Soissons

LE PRINCE DE CONDE

promised, under the sanction of the king, to assume the protectorate of the undertaking. Louis XIII listened favourably to the petition of his loyal subject, and granted the direction and control of the settlement to the count, who in due course honoured Champlain with the lieutenancy. Soon after this event, however, the count died, and His Majesty committed the direction of affairs to Monseigneur Le Prince de Condé, who retained Champlain as his lieutenant,

After having caused his commission to be posted in all the ports of Normandy, Champlain sailed from France on March 6th, in the vessel of Pont-Gravé, and arrived at Pointe aux Vaches, near Tadousac, on April 29th, 1613.

The savages came on board the vessel and inquired for Champlain. Some one replied that he had remained in France. On hearing this, an old man approached Champlain, who was walking in a corner of the vessel, and examined the scar on his ear, which was caused by an arrow wound while fighting for the Indians. On seeing this, the old man recognized Champlain, and expressed his feelings by shouts of delight, in which he was joined by his companions, who said, "Your people are awaiting you in the harbour of Tadousac."

On arriving at Tadousac, Champlain found that these Indians were almost dying of hunger, and after having affixed the arms and commission of

CHAMPLAIN

His Majesty to a post in the port, he proceeded to Quebec, which he reached on May 7th. The people of the settlement were all in good health, and the winter having been less severe than usual, the river had not frozen once.

On the 13th of the month Champlain left for the Falls of St. Louis, which he reached eight days afterwards. Here he met a number of the Algonquins, who informed him that the bad treatment which they had experienced during the previous year had discouraged them from coming to trade, and that his long absence from the country had left the whole tribe under the impression that he did not intend to return. On hearing this, Champlain recognized that it would be advisable to visit the Algonquins at once, in order to continue his discoveries, and to preserve friendly relations with them.

During his residence in France, Champlain had met a young Frenchman named Nicholas du Vignau, who claimed to have seen the Northern Sea, and said that the Ottawa River flowed from a lake which emptied into it. He also stated that the journey from Sault St. Louis to this sea and return could be accomplished in seventeen days, and that he had seen there the wreck and débris of an English ship which had contained eighty men. This intelligence seemed the more probable as the English who visited the Labrador coast in 1612, were supposed to have discovered a strait.

A VISIT TO THE ALGONQUINS

Champlain requested a merchant of La Rochelle, named Georges, to give du Vignau a passage on his ship, which he did willingly, and he also made an affidavit before a notary concerning du Vignau's Relation. Du Vignau came to Canada, and accompanied Champlain on his visit to the Algonquins. The party, consisting of four Frenchmen and one savage, set out from Ste. Helen's Island on May 27th, 1613.

After having passed the falls they entered Lake St. Louis. On the last day of May they passed Lake des Deux Montagnes, which Champlain called Lake de Soissons. Some days after thay came in sight of the river Gatineau, the river Rideau and its fall, and the Chaudière Falls, where they were forced to land. They also passed the rapid des Chats, Lake des Chats, Madawaska River, Muskrat Lake, and Allumette Island, opposite which an Algonquin chief named Tessoüat resided. On the following day the Indians gave a *tabagie* in honour of Champlain, who after smoking the pipe of peace with the party, explained to them that the object of his visit was to assure them of his friendship, and to assist them in their wars, as he had done before.[1]

[1] The day before the *tabagie* Champlain visited the Indian settlement on what has now been identified as Morrison Island, just below the Allumette Rapids. Further, an astrolabe was found on the portage to Muskrat Lake in 1867, which it seems likely was lost by Champlain when he made that difficult portage. See the excellent map and references in *The Works of Samuel de Champlain* (Champlain Society Publications), ed. H. P. Biggar, vol. ii, 1925, pp. 278, 275 notes, and Pref. viii.

CHAMPLAIN

He told them also that he was making an excursion into their country to observe the fertility of the soil, and study their lakes and rivers, and to discover the sea which he was told was in their vicinity. Champlain therefore requested them to furnish four canoes, and eight Indians as guides, to conduct the party to the Nipissirini, in order to induce them also to join in the alliance.

The chief Tessoüat, speaking in behalf of the whole tribe, said that he regarded Champlain as the most friendly of all the French, for the others were unwilling to help them in their wars, but that they had resolved not to go to the falls again, and that, owing to the long absence of Champlain from the country, they had been compelled to go to the wars alone. They therefore begged him to postpone his expedition until the following year.

They granted Champlain's request of four canoes with great reluctance, and stated that the Nipissirini were sorcerers, and not their friends. Champlain insisted on having the guides, and stated that he had brought with him a young man who would find no difficulty in visiting the country of the Nipissirini.

Tessoüat thereupon addressed the young man by name, and said: "Nicholas, is it true that you were among the Nebicerini?" "Yes," said he in Algonquin language, "I was there." "You are a downright liar," replied Tessoüat, "you know well that you slept at my side every night, with my children,

THE NIPISSIRINI

where you arose every morning; if you were among the people mentioned, it was while sleeping. How could you have been as bold as to lead your chief to believe lies, and so wicked as to be willing to expose his life to so many dangers? You are a worthless fellow and ought to be put to death, more cruelly than we do our enemies."

Shortly after, Champlain advised the Indians that the young lad had confessed that he had lied concerning his visits to the Nipissirini country. By telling them the facts Champlain hoped to save the life of Nicholas du Vignau, as the savages had said, "Give him to us, and we promise that he shall not lie any more."

On June 10th Champlain took leave of Tessoüat, after making him presents and promising to return during the next year to assist in the war. Returning on his course, Champlain again approached the Chaudière Falls, where the savages went through a ceremony peculiar to them, which is thus described:

"After carrying their canoes to the foot of the falls, they assembled in one spot, where one of them took up a collection in a wooden plate, into which each one placed a piece of tobacco. The collection having been made, the plate was placed in the middle of the troupe, and they all danced around it, singing after their style. Then one of them made a harangue, setting forth that for a long time they had been accustomed to make this offering, by means of which they were insured

CHAMPLAIN

protection against their enemies, and that otherwise misfortune would befall them, as they were convinced by the evil spirit; and that they lived on in this superstition, as in many others. This done, the maker of the harangue took the plate, and threw the tobacco into the midst of the caldron, whereupon they all raised a loud cry."

Such was the superstition of these savages that they considered a favourable journey impossible without this uncouth ceremony. It was at this portage that their enemies had been wont to surprise them.

On June 17th they arrived at Sault St. Louis on their return journey. Captain L'Ange, who was the confidant of Champlain, brought news that Maisonneuve of St. Malo had arrived with a passport from the Prince de Condé for three vessels. Champlain therefore allowed him to trade with the savages.

As the trade with the savages was now completed, Champlain resolved to return to France by the first vessel which was ready to start. He accepted a passage in Maisonneuve's vessel, which arrived at St. Malo on August 26th. Champlain had an interview with the merchants, to whom he represented that a good association could be formed in the future. The merchants resolved to follow the example of those of Rouen and La Rochelle.

In concluding this chapter we may repeat the words with which Champlain ends his account

IN FRANCE AGAIN, 1613

of his voyage of this year: "May God by His grace cause this undertaking to prosper to His honour and glory to the conversion of these poor benighted ones, and to honour and welfare of France."[1]

[1] Champlain's voyages from 1604-13 are contained in two parts:—
Les Voyages du Sieur de Champlain Xaintongeois, capitaine pour le Roy en la Marine . . . a Paris, MDCXIII. This volume contains a letter to the King, another to the Queen, stanzas addressed to the French, an ode to Champlain on his books and his marine maps signed by Motin. The first book contains the voyages of Champlain along the coasts of Acadia and New England. The second relates to the voyages of Champlain to Quebec, in the years 1608, 1610 and 1611.
Quatrième voyage du Sr. de Champlain, capitaine ordinaire pour le Roy en la Marine, et Lieutenant de Monseigneur le Prince de Condé en la Nouvelle France, fait en l'année 1613. This volume contains a letter to Henri de Condé, and a geographical map, made in 1612, of a large size and very curious. The history of this voyage is really a part of the so-called edition of 1613, and the printing of it was done at the same time as the Relations of the first, second and third voyages, which form altogether a large volume of three hundred and twenty-five pages.

Translations of both these parts are to be found in vols. i and ii of the Champlain Society edition of his works, and also in W. L. Grant's edition.

CHAPTER V

THE RÉCOLLETS AND THEIR MISSIONS

CHAMPLAIN'S affection for New France, the land of his adoption, made him anxious to continue his explorations, in order that he might become familiar with every locality. In the course of his voyages he often had to be conveyed in Indian canoes, especially on the lakes and rivers, but this means was sufficient only when his object was to ascertain whether the country was well watered, whether the rivers were more or less navigable, whether the lakes abounded with fish, and whether the water powers were capable of being turned to account. Up till this time the founder of Quebec had pressed forward his work of exploration with an energy that was almost astonishing. He had rowed up the Iroquois River as far as lake Champlain, and he had also navigated the Ottawa River in a manner that had even surprised the Algonquins. Still many things remained to be done and to be seen, such as to observe the fertility of the soil in different latitudes, to study the manners and customs of the Indians, especially of the great Huron tribe, which was the most populous and probably better disposed to receive Christian instruction than the other tribes. Champlain's ambition had always been to introduce Christianity in order to civilize the people. Thus we find in his writings after his return to France in 1616, the words:

"Without losing courage, I have not ceased to push on and visit various nations of the savages, and by associating familiarly with them, I have concluded, as well from their conversation as from the knowledge attained, that there is no better way than, disregarding all storms and difficulties, to have patience until His Majesty shall give the requisite attention to the matter, and in the meantime to continue the exploration of the country, but also to learn the language, and form relations and friendship with the leading men of the villages and tribes, in order to lay the foundations of a permanent edifice, as well for the glory of God as for the renown of the French."

It is well to observe the significance of these words from the pen of Champlain. Is this the language of a common fur-trader, simply seeking to increase his fortune? What were really Champlain's designs during all these years of labour and self-sacrifice? Was he animated by the mere curiosity of the tourist, or the ambition of a man of science? No. Champlain desired, it is true, to gain an intimate knowledge of the country, and his labours are highly valued as a geographer and cosmographer, but his intention was to utilize all his varied information to promote the Christian religion and at the same time to increase the renown of his native land.

THE RÉCOLLETS

Champlain deserves credit, not only for the idea of bringing missionaries to Canada, but also for having realized his ideas. He obtained the coöperation of many pious and zealous persons in France, who willingly seconded his efforts, but it was owing to his own steadfastness of purpose and to his great ability that his designs were successfully carried out. After having formed a society of merchants to take the material affairs of the colony in hand, Champlain tried to get some religious order to assume the direction of spiritual matters. He had previously made known his plan to Louis Hoüel, king's councillor, and comptroller of the salt works at Brouage, and sieur of Petit-Pré. Hoüel was an honourable and pious man, and a friend of Champlain. He told him that he was acquainted with some Récollets who would readily agree to proceed to New France. Hoüel met Father du Verger, a man of great virtue and ability, and principal of the order of the Immaculate Conception. Father du Verger made an appeal to his confrères, all of whom offered their services, and were ready to cross the ocean.

The cardinals and bishops who were then gathered at St. Denis for their great chapter, were in favour of the idea of sending the Récollets to their foreign missions, and promised to raise a fund for the maintenance of four monks, and the merchants of Rouen promised to maintain and convey at least six Récollets gratuitously. The king issued letters for the future church of Canada. The pope's nuncio, Guido Bentivoglio, granted the requisite permission, in conformity with the pope's wishes, but the bull establishing the church was only forwarded on May 20th, 1618. The brief of Paul V granted to the Récollets the following privileges:

"To receive all children born of believing and unbelieving parents, and all others of what condition soever they may be, who, after promising to keep and observe all that should be kept and observed by the faithful, will embrace the truth of the Christian and Catholic faith; to baptize even outside of the churches in case of necessity; to hear confessions of penitents, and after diligently hearing them, to impose a salutary penance according to their faults, and enjoin what should be enjoined in conscience, to loose and absolve them from all sentences of excommunication and other ecclesiastical pains and censures, as also from all sorts of crimes, excesses, and delicts; to administer the sacraments of the eucharist, marriage and extreme unction; to bless all kinds of vestments, vessels and ornaments when holy unction is not necessary; to dispense gratuitously new converts who have contracted or would contract marriage in any degree of consanguinity, or affinity whatever, except the first or second, or between ascending and descending, provided the women have not been carried off by force, and the two parties who have contracted or would contract be Catholics, and there be just cause as

FOUNDERS OF THE MISSION

well for the marriages already contracted as for those desired to be contracted; to declare and pronounce the children born and issued of such marriages legitimate; to have an altar which they may decently carry, and thereon to celebrate in decent and becoming places where the convenience of a church shall be wanting."

The Reverend Father Garnier de Chapouin, provincial of the province of St. Denis, appointed four monks as the founders of the future mission. Their names were Father Denis Jamet, Jean d'Olbeau, Joseph Le Caron, and a brother named Pacifique du Plessis, who received orders to accompany them. These four monks were all remarkable for their virtue and apostolic zeal. Father Jamet was appointed commissary, and Father d'Olbeau was appointed his successor in the event of death. The king granted them authority to build one or more convents in Canada, and to send for as many monks as were required. It was impossible to send more than four of them during the first year.

On April 24th, 1615, the *St. Étienne* sailed from Honfleur, and one month later came to anchor at Tadousac. On June 25th, Father d'Olbeau was able to say mass in a small chapel built at the foot of Mountain Hill, Quebec.

Soon after his arrival at Quebec, Champlain set out for the falls, accompanied by Father Jamet. They reached the river des Prairies some days after, and on June 24th, Father Jamet celebrated a solemn

CHAMPLAIN

mass, at which Champlain and some others assisted. This was the first mass celebrated in Canada since the days of Jacques Cartier.

In the early days of the settlement these brave missionaries had to contend with many difficulties, which could be foreseen only by those who were acquainted with the existing state of affairs. Many of these difficulties arose from the fact that at least a fourth of the merchants of the company were members of the so-called reformed, or Calvinistic persuasion. It is easy to comprehend that the sympathies of these men would not incline towards the Catholic religion.

Champlain draws particular attention to the unfortunate results produced by the existence of different creeds. Differences arose, and divisions were created which sometimes resulted in quarrels between children of the same country. These quarrels which were much to be deplored, did not, however, occur in Quebec, because the French merchants did not deem it advisable to send their ministers there, but replaced them by agents who were often fanatical, and were for the Récollets a frequent source of bitterness and annoyance. The most of the disorders occurred on board the vessels, and were due to the fact that the crews were too hastily engaged.

The merchants, however, were bound to colonize the country with Catholic settlers, and de Monts was also bound by similar conditions. Moreover,

THE RÉCOLLETS' DIFFICULTIES

the terms of the patents expressly stipulated that this should be carried out. They were also forbidden to extend Calvinism among the savages. "This policy," says Bancroft, "was full of wisdom." The interpreters who could have greatly assisted the missionaries, proved on the contrary an obstacle to the development of the Catholic religion, for they refused to instruct the Récollets in the Indian languages, which they had learnt before the arrival of the missionaries.

Father Lalemant, a Jesuit, wrote in the year 1626: "This interpreter had never wanted to communicate his knowledge of the language to any one, not even to the Reverend Récollet Fathers, who had constantly importuned him for ten years." So also wrote Father Le Jeune in his Relation of 1633.

The difficulties that the missionaries had to overcome are therefore readily understood. However they had the merit of preparing the way for their successors, and the honour of planting the cross of Jesus Christ everywhere, from Tadousac to Lake Huron.

The number of missionaries was limited at the commencement, but some others came to Canada later, particularly Fathers Guillaume Poullain, Georges Le Baillif, and Paul Huet. These men, some of whom were of noble birth, were remarkable for their virtues and their abilities. In the annals of the primitive church of New France, their names are illustrious, and around their memory gathers

CHAMPLAIN

the aureole of sanctity. During six years, from 1615 to 1621, the spiritual direction of the colony was entrusted to six fathers and three friars. Father d'Olbeau remained in charge of the habitation of Quebec, and Father Le Caron resolved to proceed at once to the country of the Hurons.

On July 9th, 1615, Champlain, Etienne Brûlé, an interpreter, a servant, and ten Indians, set out for the mouth of the Ottawa River. They rowed up the river as far as the Mattawa, which they followed westwards, and soon reached Lake Nipissing where they stopped for two days. This was on July 26th. After having taken this short rest, they continued their voyage, crossing Georgian Bay, and reached the land of the Hurons. Near the shore they met the Attignaouantans, or people of the bear tribe, one of the four chief branches of the great Huron family. Their village or *bourgade* was called Otouacha. On the second day of August, Champlain's party visited the village of Carmaron, and two days later, they saw the encampments of Tonaguainchain Tequenonquiayé and Carhagouha. In the latter emcampment Father Le Caron resided.

On July 12th Father Le Caron celebrated mass and sang the *Te Deum*, after which the Indians planted a cross near the small chapel which had been erected under Champlain's direction. The reverend father occupied a hut within the palisade which formed the rampart of the village, and he

THE HURON COUNTRY

spent the fall and winter with the Hurons of Carhagouha.

The Huron country was situated between the peninsula watered by Lake Simcoe on the eastern side, and by the Georgian Bay on the western side. It extended from north to south between the rivers Severn and Nottawasaga. This land is twenty-five leagues in length and seven or eight in width. The soil, though sandy, was fertile and produced in abundance corn, beans, pumpkins and the annual helianthus or sun-flower, from which the Hurons extracted the oil. The neighbouring tribes, such as the Ottawas and the Algonquins, used to procure their provisions from the Hurons, as they were permanently cultivating their lands.

Champlain observed, in 1615, that there were eighteen *bourgades* or villages, of which he mentions five, namely: Carhagouha, Toanché, Carmeron, Tequenonquiayé and Cahiagué. Cahiagué was the most important, and had two hundred huts; it was also the chief *bourgade* of the tribe called de la Roche.

Four tribes of a common origin and a common language were living on the Huron peninsula. They were: (1.) The Attignaouantans, or Tribe de l'Ours; (2.) The Attignenonghacs, or Tribe de la Corde; (3.) The Arendarrhonons, or Tribe de la Roche; (4.) The Tohontahenrats. The general name given to these four tribes by the French was Ouendats.

The most numerous and the most respected of the tribes were the tribes de l'Ours and de la Corde, which had taken possession of the country; the first about the year 1589, and the second twenty years after. The oldest men of these tribes related to the missionaries, in 1638, that their ancestors for the past two hundred years had been obliged to change their residence every ten years. These two tribes were very friendly, and in their councils treated each other like brothers. All their business was conducted through the medium of a captain of war and a captain of council.

These tribes became popular and increased their numbers by adopting members of other nations, so that in later years the Huron family became one of the most powerful and redoubtable in North America. The identity of language was a great factor in the accomplishment of this marvellous result. The Andastes, of the Susquehanna, for instance, spoke a language akin to the Huron. The Tionnontatés became so identified with their neighbours that they were named the Hurons of the Petun. The savages of the Neutral Nation had also adopted the Huron idiom. This uniformity of language formed a league between these nations which would have been broken with the utmost difficulty.

Father de Brébeuf calculated that, in his time, there were scattered over the whole continent of North America about three hundred thousand Indians who understood the Huron dialect. This was exaggerated, for the aborigines covering the territory known to the Hurons from whom the father

THE IROQUOIS TRIBE

had collected this information did not number three hundred thousand persons. How could he rely upon these people, to whom a thousand men represented simply an amazing number? How could the Hurons make a census of an unsedentary people, wandering here and there according to circumstances of war or other reasons, and recruiting themselves with prisoners or with the remnants of conquered nations?

To give only one example of these strange recruitings, let us examine the composition of the great family of the Iroquois in Champlain's time. It was a collection of disbanded tribes, who had belonged to the Hurons, to the Tionnontatés, to the Neutral, to the Eries and du Feu tribes. The Iroquois had separated themselves from the Hurons to form a branch which acquired with time more virility than the tree from which it had sprung. The Hurons were called the good Iroquois in order to distinguish them from the wicked Iroquois who were reputed to be barbarous. These fought against all the nations living in Canada, and their name was a subject of general apprehension.

Returning to the Hurons, we find that the Attignaouantans, or the tribe de l'Ours, was the most populous, forming half of the whole Huron family, namely about fifteen thousand souls. They were considered, erroneously, as the most perfidious of all. Father de Brébeuf, who knew them well, says that they were mild, charitable, polite and

CHAMPLAIN

courteous. Some years later, the tribe de l'Ours occupied fourteen villages, with thirteen missions under the charge of the Jesuits. The whole mission, called Immaculate Conception, had its principal seat at Ossossané, which had replaced Carhagouha, mentioned by Champlain. The French called it La Rochelle. Ossossané was the nearest village of the Iroquois territory. Father du Creux' map places it on the western coast of the Huron peninsula.

The Attignenonghacs, or tribe de la Corde, were the oldest and the most numerous, after the Attignaouantans. They praised their antiquity and their traditions which had existed for two hundred years, and which had been collected by word of mouth by the chiefs or captains. This evidence, more or less valuable, seems to indicate that they had preserved a family spirit, which is very laudable. The Attignenonghacs, however, had founded a nationality, and their language was so developed that, in 1635, Father de Brébeuf could recall to memory twelve nations who spoke it. This tribe had no special features except that they were very devoted to the French. The Jesuits opened in their midst two missions called St. Ignace and St. Joseph. Teanaustayaé was one of the most important villages of the Attignenonghacs. When the village of Ihonatiria ceased to exist, the Jesuits called it St. Joseph. Here perished, in 1648, Father Daniel, together with seven hundred Hurons.

INDIAN SETTLEMENTS

Toanché was another village of the same tribe. It has often changed its name, and we may consider it as one of these flying *bourgades* so commonly found among the Hurons. Champlain had known the village of Toanché under the name of Otouacha. When Father de Brébeuf came here for the second time, in 1634, he was unable to recognize the village that he had visited for the first time in 1626. It had been transported about two miles from its former place. It was then situated at the western entrance of a bay now Penetanguishene, on a point in the northern part of Lake Huron, four leagues from Ossossané and seven from Teanaustayaé.

The Arendarrhonons, or tribe de la Roche, were settled on the eastern part of the peninsula. They were at first discovered by the French, and they had, according to the laws of the country, the privilege of fur trading. They were especially attached to Champlain, and twenty-two years after his death they had not forgotten his remarkable virtues and courage. The *bourgade* of Cahiagué, comprising two hundred and sixty huts and two thousand souls, was the chief place of the Arendarrhonons. It was situated near the lake Ouentaron, now lake Simcoe, at the northern extremity, near the small town of Orillia. The Jesuits established a mission here, and their principal residence was on the right shore of a small river called the Wye, near Penetanguishene. The remains of a fort built there in 1639 could be seen a few years ago.

CHAMPLAIN

Cahiagué was distant from Carhagouha fourteen leagues. It was situated near the village of Scanonahenrat, where the Tohontahenrats, the fourth Huron tribe, resided. They were less numerous than the others. Scanonahenrat was situated at about two leagues from Ihonatiria of the Attignenonghacs, and at three leagues from the Ataronchronons, another Huron group of small importance, where finally the Jesuits took up their residence. When these missions were flourishing, the Jesuits could enumerate twenty-five different places where they could pursue their calling with zeal. The Récollets had continued their course with vigorous activity; they had sown the divine seed, but they were not permitted to reap the reward of their labours, as the Jesuits did in the future.

Although the Hurons appeared to be happy, their mode of living was miserable. Their principal articles of food were Indian corn and common beans, which they prepared in various ways. Their clothing was made of the skins of wild animals. Deer skin was used for their trousers, which were cut loose, and their stockings were made of another piece of the same skin, while their boots were formed of the skin of bears, beavers and deer. They also wore a cloak in the Egyptian style, with sleeves which were attached by a string behind. Most of them painted their faces black and red, and dyed their hair, which some wore long, others short, and others again on one side only. The women and girls were

THE HURONS

dressed like men, except that they had their robes, which extended to the knee, girt about them. They all dressed their hair in one uniform style, carefully combed, dyed and oiled. For ornaments they wore quantities of porcelain, chains and necklaces, besides bracelets and ear-rings.

These people were of a happy temperament generally, though some had a sad and gloomy countenance. Physically they were well proportioned. Some of the men and women had fine figures, strong and robust, and many of the women were powerful and of unusual height. The greater portion of the work fell to the lot of the women, who looked after the housework, tilled the land, laid up a store of wood for the winter, beat the hemp and spun it, and made fishing nets from the thread. They also gathered in the harvest and prepared it for food. The occupation of the men was hunting for deer, fishing, and building their cabins, varied at times by war. When they were free from these occupations, they visited other tribes with whom they were acquainted for the purpose of traffic or exchange, and their return was celebrated by dances and festivities.

They had a certain form of marriage which Champlain thus describes. When a girl had reached the age of eleven, twelve, thirteen, fourteen or fifteen years, she had suitors, more or less, according to her attractions, who wooed her for some time. The consent of the parents was then asked, to whose wills the girl did not always submit, although the most discreet of them did so. The favoured lover or suitor then presented to the girl some necklaces, bracelets or chains of porcelain, which she accepted if the suitor was agreeable to her. The suitor then resided with her for three or four days, without saying anything to her in the meantime, but if they did not agree, the girl left her suitor, who forfeited his necklaces and the other presents which he had made, and each was free to seek another companion if so disposed. This term of probation was often extended to eight, or even to fifteen days.

The children enjoyed great freedom. The parents indulged them too much and never punished or corrected them. As a consequence they grew up bad and vicious. They would often strike their mothers, and when they were powerful enough they did not hesitate to strike their fathers.

The Hurons did not recognize any divine power or worship of God. They were without belief, and lived like brute beasts, with this exception, that they had a sort of fear of an evil spirit. They had *ogni* or *manitous*, who were medicine-men, and who healed the sick, bound up the wounded, foretold future events, and practised all the abuses and illusions of the black arts.

Champlain firmly believed that the conversion of the Hurons to Christianity would have been easier if the country had been inhabited by persons who

HURONS ANXIOUS TO IMPROVE

would devote their energies to instructing them. Father Le Caron and himself had often conversed with them regarding the Catholic faith, the laws and customs of the French, and they had listened attentively, sometimes saying:

"You say things that pass our knowledge, and which we cannot understand by words, being beyond our comprehension; but if you would do us a service, come and dwell in this country, bringing your wives and children, and when they are here, we shall see how you serve the God you worship, and how you live with your wives and children, how you cultivate and plant the soil, how you obey your laws, how you take care of animals, and how you manufacture all that we see proceeding from your inventive skill. When we see all this we shall learn more in a year than in twenty by simply hearing your discourse; and if we cannot understand, you shall take our children, who shall be as your own. And thus being convinced that our life is a miserable one in comparison with yours, it is easy to believe that we shall adopt yours, abandoning our own."

The following was their mode of government. The older and leading men assembled in a council, in which they settled upon and proposed all that was necessary for the affairs of the village. This was done by a plurality of voices, or in accordance with the advice of some one among them whose judgment they considered superior; such a one was requested by the company to give his opinion on the propositions that had been made, and his opinion was minutely obeyed. They had no particular chief with absolute command, but they honoured the older and more courageous men, of which there were several in a village, whom they named captains, as a mark of distinction and respect.

They all deliberated in common, and whenever any member of the assembly offered to do anything for the welfare of the village, or to go anywhere for the service of the community, he was requested to present himself, and if he was judged capable of carrying out what he proposed, they exhorted him, by fair and favourable words, to do his duty. They declared him to be an energetic man, fit for the undertaking, and assured him that he would win honour in accomplishing his task. In a word, they encouraged him by flatteries, in order that this favourable disposition of his for the welfare of his fellow-citizens might continue and increase. Then, according to his pleasure, he accepted or refused the responsibility, and thereby he was held in high esteem.

They had, moreover, general assemblies with representatives from remote regions. These representatives came every year, one from each province, and met in a town designated as the rendezvous of the assembly. Here were celebrated great banquets and dances, for three weeks or a month, according as they might determine. On these occasions they

THE BURIAL OF THE DEAD

renewed their friendship, resolved upon and decreed what they thought best for the preservation of their country against their enemies, and made each other handsome presents, after which they retired to their own districts.

In burying the dead, the Hurons took the body of the deceased, wrapped it in furs, and covered it very carefully with the bark of trees. Then they placed it in a cabin, of the length of the body, made of bark and erected upon four posts. Others they placed in the ground, propping up the earth on all sides that it might not fall on the body, which they covered with the bark of trees, putting earth on top. Over this trench they also made a little cabin. The bodies remained thus buried for a period of eight or ten years. Then they held a general council, to which all the people of the country were invited, for the purpose of determining upon some place for the holding of a great festival. After this they returned each to his own village, where they took all the bones of the deceased, stripped them and made them quite clean. These they kept very carefully, although the odour arising therefrom was noxious. Then all the relatives and friends of the deceased took these bones, together with their necklaces, furs, axes, kettles, and other things highly valued, and carried them, with a quantity of edibles, to the place assigned. Here, when all had assembled, they put the edibles in a place designated by the men of the village, and engaged in banquets and continual dancing. The festival lasted for the space of ten days, during which other tribes from all quarters came to witness the ceremonies. The latter were attended with great outlays.

These details on the manners and customs of the Hurons are quoted nearly *verbatim* from Champlain's Relations, so they must be considered as accurate.[1]

[1] This is the volume which Champlain issued after his return to France in the year 1618. It was entitled *Voyages et Déscouvertures faites en la Nouvelle France depuis l'année 1615, jusques à la fin de l'année 1618.* Par le Sieur de Champlain, Capitaine ordinaire pour le Roy en la Mer de Ponant, MDCXIX. An English translation is given in the volume containing the *Voyages* 1604-18, ed. W. L. Grant, already referred to.

CHAPTER VI

WAR AGAINST THE IROQUOIS, 1615

CHAMPLAIN had promised for some years to assist the Hurons in their wars against the Iroquois, and he found that the present time was opportune for him to fulfil his pledge. He had visited every Huron tribe, and he was aware that a general rendezvous had been fixed at Cahiagué. On August 14th, 1615, ten Frenchmen, under the command of Champlain, started from Carhagouha. On their way they stopped at the villages of the Tohontahenrats and Attignenonghacs, and found the country well watered and cultivated, and the villages populous. The people, however, were ignorant, avaricious and untruthful, and had no idea either of a divinity or of a religion.

On August 17th, Champlain came in sight of Cahiagué, where the Hurons had gathered, and after some hesitation, they decided to go to war. The departure was delayed until September 1st, pending the arrival of some of their warriors and the Andastes, who had promised five hundred men. On their journey they passed by Lake Couchiching and Lake Ouantaron or Simcoe. From there they decided to proceed by way of Sturgeon Lake, after travelling by land for a distance of ten leagues.

CHAMPLAIN

From Sturgeon Lake flows the river Otonabee, which discharges into Rice Lake.

They followed the river Trent to the Bay of Quinté in Lake Ontario or Entouronotons. "Here," says Champlain, "is the entrance of the great river of St. Lawrence." They leisurely crossed Lake Ontario, and, having hidden their canoes, penetrated the woods and crossed the river Chouagen or Oswego, which flows from Lake Oneida where the Iroquois used to fish.

On October 9th the Hurons had approached within four leagues of the fortifications of their enemies, and on that day eleven Iroquois fell into the hands of Champlain's men, and were made prisoners. Iroquet, the chief of the Petite Nation, prepared to torture the prisoners, among whom were four women and four children, but Champlain strongly opposed this course. The Iroquois were engaged in reaping their corn when the Hurons and their allies appeared before them on October 10th, or five weeks after Champlain had started from Cahiagué. During this period Champlain's army had undergone much fatigue, and it was desirable to take some rest.

The first day was spent in petty skirmishes. Instead of fighting in ranks, the Hurons disbanded, and were consequently liable to be seized by the vigilance of their enemies. Champlain recognized the danger of this method of warfare, and persuaded his companions to preserve their ranks. The last

THE RETREAT

combat continued for about three hours, during which Ochateguin and Orani, two of the allied chiefs, were wounded. Champlain also received two arrow wounds, one in the leg and one in the knee. There was great disorder in the ranks of the Hurons, and the chiefs had no control over their men. The result, on the whole, was not in favour of Champlain's allies, who in the absence of the Andastes were not anxious to continue the attacks against the Iroquois, and consequently determined to retreat as soon as possible.

Champlain suffered much from his wounds. " I never found myself in such a gehenna," he says, "as during this time, for the pain which I suffered in consequence of the wound in my knee was nothing in comparison with that which I endured while I was carried, bound and pinioned, on the back of one of the savages."

The retreat was very long, and on October 18th they arrived at the shore of Lake Ontario. Here Champlain requested that he might have a canoe and guides to conduct him to Quebec, as this was one of the conditions to which they had agreed before he set out for the war. The Indians were not to be trusted, however, and they refused his request. Champlain, therefore, resolved to accept the hospitality of Darontal, chief of the Arendarrhonons, or tribe de la Roche. The chief appeared kindly disposed towards Champlain, and as it was the hunting season, he accompanied him on his excursions. During one of these expeditions, Champlain lost his way in the pursuit of a strange bird, and he was not found by the savages until three days afterwards. The return journey to Cahiagué on foot was painful, and during the nineteen days thus spent, much hardship was undergone. The party arrived at Cahiagué on December 23rd, 1615.

In the course of the winter, Champlain was chosen to act as judge of a quarrel between the Algonquins of the Petite Nation, and the Hurons of the tribe de l'Ours, which had arisen over the murder of one of the Iroquois. The Attignaouantans had committed an Iroquois prisoner to the custody of Iroquet, requesting him to burn him according to their custom. Instead of carrying out this act, Iroquet had taken the young man and treated him as a son. When the Attignaouantans were aware of this, they sent one of their number to murder the young Iroquois. This barbarous conduct made the Algonquins indignant, and they killed the murderer.

Champlain returned from the Petuneux in company with Father Le Caron at the time when these crimes had just been committed. Witnesses were summoned to meet Champlain at Cahiagué, and were each examined. The trial lasted two days, during which the old men of both nations were consulted, and the majority of them were favourable to a reconciliation without conditions. Champlain exacted from them a promise that they would ac-

HIS ADDRESS

cept his decision as final, and he then had a full meeting of the two tribes assembled there. Addressing them, he said:

"You Algonquins, and you Hurons, have always been friends. You have lived like brothers; you take this name in your councils. Your conduct now is unworthy of reasonable men. You are enough occupied in repelling your enemies, who have pursued you, who rout you as often as possible, pursuing you to your villages and taking you prisoners. These enemies, seeing these divisions and wars among you, will be delighted and derive great advantage therefrom. On account of the death of one man you will hazard the lives of ten thousand, and run the risk of being reduced to perpetual slavery. Although in fact one man was of great value, you ought to consider how he has been killed; it was not with deliberate purpose, nor for the sake of inciting a civil war. The Algonquins much regret all that has taken place, and if they had supposed such a thing would have happened, they would have sacrificed this Iroquois for the satisfaction of the Hurons. Forget all, never think of it again, but live good friends as before. In case you should not be pleased with my advice, I request you to come in as large numbers as possible, to our settlement, so that there, in presence of all the captains of vessels, the friendship might be ratified anew, and measures taken to secure you from your enemies."

CHAMPLAIN

Champlain's advice was followed, and the savages went away satisfied, except the Algonquins, who broke up and proceeded to their villages, saying that the death of these two men had cost them too dearly.

Champlain having spent the winter with Darontal, on May 20th left for Quebec. The journey from Cahiagué to Sault St. Louis occupied forty days. Champlain here found that Pont-Gravé had arrived from France with two vessels, and that the reverend fathers were very pleased to see him again. Darontal accompanied Champlain to Quebec, and greatly admired the habitation and the mode of living adopted by the French. Before leaving for France, Champlain enlarged the habitation by at least one-third, the additions consisting of buildings and fortifications, in the construction of which he used lime and sand which were found near at hand. Some grain was also cut, and the gardens were left in good condition.

During the winter of 1615-16, Father Le Caron had received a visit from Champlain, who had just returned from an expedition against the Iroquois. Being anxious to see as many Indian tribes as possible, Champlain and the Récollet resolved to pay a visit to the Tionnontatés, or the Tobacco Nation. The missionary was not well received by these people, although Champlain was able to make an alliance, not only with the Petuneux, but also with six or seven other tribes living in the vicinity.

LE CARON AND D'OLBEAU

Father Le Caron returned to his flock, the Hurons, and remained with them until May 20th, studying their manners, trying to acquire their language, and to improve their morals. Father Le Clercq says that he compiled a dictionary which was seen in his own time, and which was preserved as a relic.

When the Hurons left their country to engage in fur trading with the French at Sault St. Louis, Father Le Caron took passage in one of their canoes, and arrived at Three Rivers on July 1st, 1616. Here he met Father d'Olbeau, who had spent the winter with the Indians on the north shore of the river St. Lawrence, between Tadousac and the Seven Islands.

Father d'Olbeau had visited the Bersiamites, the Papinachois and others, and he planted crosses everywhere, so that many years after, when some Frenchmen were visiting the place, they found these evidences of his labours. After two months of fatigue, Father d'Olbeau was compelled to return to Quebec, as he was suffering from sore eyes, and was unable to unclose his eyelids for several weeks. The two fathers arrived at Quebec on July 11th, 1616, and Father Jamet was pleased to learn the result of the missions of his confrères. The three missionaries had carefully studied the country during the past year, and gained a fair knowledge of the people. They realized at this time that their own resources limited their power of doing good,

CHAMPLAIN

and they therefore requested Champlain to convoke a meeting of six inhabitants, to discuss the best means of furthering the interests of the mission. Champlain was chosen president of the meeting, and although the missionaries were present they took no part in the deliberations.

The resolutions adopted at this first council meeting in the new settlement were preserved. It was decided that the nations down the river and those of the north were, for the present, at least, incapable of civilization. These tribes included the Montagnais, Etchemins, Bersiamites, Papinachois and the great and little Esquimaux. They dwelt in an uncultivated, barren and mountainous country, whose wild game and fur-bearing animals sufficed to support them. Their habits were nomadic, and excessive superstition was their only form of religion. By the report of those who had visited the southern coasts, and had even penetrated by land to Cadie, Cape Breton and Chaleurs Bay, Ile Percé and Gaspé, the country there was more temperate, and susceptible of cultivation. There would be found dispositions less estranged from Christianity, as the people had more shame, docility and humanity than the others.

With regard to the upper river and the territory of the numerous tribes of Indians visited by Monsieur de Champlain and Father Joseph themselves, or by others, besides possessing an abundance of game, which might attract the French there in hopes of trade, the land was much more fertile and

THE UPPER RIVER INDIANS

the climate more congenial than in the Indian country down the river. The upper river Indians, such as the Algonquins, Iroquois, Hurons, Nipissirini, Neuters, Fire Nation, were sedentary, generally docile, susceptible of instruction, charitable, strong, robust, patient; insensible, however, and indifferent to all that concerns salvation; lascivious, and so material that when told that their soul was immortal, they would ask what they would eat after death in the next world. In general, none of the savages whom they had known had any idea of a divinity, believing, nevertheless, in another world where they hoped to enjoy the same pleasures as they took here below—a people, in short, without subordination, law or form of government or system, gross in religious matters, shrewd and crafty for trade and profit, but superstitious to excess.

It was the opinion of the council that none could ever succeed in converting them, unless they made them men before they made them Christians. To civilize them it was necessary first that the French should mingle with them and habituate them to their presence and mode of life, which could be done only by the increase of the colony, the greatest obstacle to which was on the part of the gentlemen of the company, who, to monopolize trade, did not wish the country to be settled, and did not even wish to make the Indians sedentary, which was the only condition favourable to the salvation of these heathen.

CHAMPLAIN

The Protestants, or Huguenots, having the best share in the trade, it was to be feared that the contempt they showed for the Catholic mysteries would greatly retard the establishment of that faith. Even the bad example of the French might be prejudicial, if those who had authority in the country did not establish order.

The mission among such numerous nations would be painful and laborious, and so could advance but little unless they obtained from the gentlemen of the company a greater number of missionaries free of expense. Even then it would require many years and great labour to humanize these utterly gross and barbarous nations, and even when this end was partially attained, the sacrament, for fear of profanation, could be administered only to an exceptional few among the adults.

It finally appears to have been decided that they could not make progress unless the colony was increased by a greater number of settlers, mechanics and farmers; that free trade with the Indians should be permitted, without distinction, to all Frenchmen; that in future Huguenots should be excluded, and that it was necessary to render the Indians sedentary, and bring them up to a knowledge of French manners and laws.

The council further agreed that by the help of zealous persons in France, a seminary ought to be established in order to bring to Christianity, young Indians, who might afterwards aid the mis-

LACK OF RELIGIOUS INTEREST

sionaries in converting their countrymen. It was deemed necessary to maintain the missions which the fathers had established both up and down the river. This could not be done unless the associated gentlemen showed all the ardour to be expected from their zeal when informed of all things faithfully, instead of being deluded by the reports of the clerks whom they had sent the year before; the governor and the fathers having no ground to be satisfied therewith.

Champlain, who intended to return to France, desired the father commissary and Father Le Caron to accompany him, in order that the resolutions of the council might be submitted to the king for his approval, and with a view of obtaining substantial assistance. The voyage was a pleasant one, and Champlain and his party arrived at Honfleur on September 10th, 1616.

The merchants whom they interviewed at Paris were ready to promise to support the mission, but nothing was realized from their promises, and it soon became apparent that they cared more about the fur trade than about religion. Champlain saw many people who he believed could assist the settlement, but the winter was passed in useless negotiations. He therefore prepared a greater shipment than usual from his own resources, and he was fortunate in finding that his old friend, Louis Hébert, an apothecary of Port Royal, was willing to accompany him. Hébert took his family with him, composed of three children and his wife, named Marie Rollet. Hébert afterwards rendered very valuable assistance to the founder of Quebec.

Father Jamet did not return to Quebec, and he was therefore replaced as commissary by Father Le Caron, who appointed Father Huet as his assistant. The vessel conveying the party sailed from Honfleur on March 11th, 1617, under the command of Captain Morel. The passage was very rough, and when within sixty leagues of the Great Bank of Newfoundland, numerous icebergs bore down on the ship like huge mountains. Father Le Clerq says that in the general consternation Father Joseph, seeing that all human succour could not deliver them from shipwreck, earnestly implored the aid of heaven in the vows and prayers which he made publicly on the vessel. He confessed all, and prepared himself to appear before God. All were touched with compassion and deeply moved when Dame Hébert raised her youngest child through the hatchway to let it share with the rest the good father's blessing. They escaped only by a miracle, as they acknowledged in their letters to France.

The ship arrived at Tadousac on June 14th, and mass was said in a little chapel which Father Huet had constructed with poles and branches, and a sailor stood on either side of the altar with fir branches to drive away the cloud of mosquitoes which caused great annoyance to the celebrant. The mass was very solemn. Besides the French,

FATHER D'OLBEAU VISITS FRANCE

there were many Indians present who assisted with devotion amid the roar of the cannon of the ship, and the muskets of the French. After the service a dinner was given by the captain on board the vessel. On the arrival of the party at Quebec some days after, they found that the inhabitants were nearly starving, and that Father d'Olbeau was anxiously awaiting the news from France.

Both Champlain and Father Le Caron were obliged to confess that their mission had been unsuccessful. What, therefore, was to be done? To return to Old France would have been contrary to the intentions of the Récollets. They had been sent to Canada by their superiors, and they had no order to act contrary to their instructions. After having studied the situation they resolved that Father d'Olbeau should visit France, see the king in person, and place before him the settlers' condition and their own. During his absence Father Huet undertook the charge of the mission at Tadousac, and Brother Pacifique du Plessis was appointed to teach catechism to the Indians of Three Rivers.

It was at about this time that Father Le Caron performed the first marriage ceremony in Canada, the contracting parties being Étienne Jonquest of Normandy, and Anne Hébert, eldest daughter of Louis Hébert.

The condition of the Récollets at this time was unenviable. The agents of the merchants were not better disposed towards them than the interpreters.

CHAMPLAIN

Some of these agents were demoralized, and the reproach that they received from the fathers caused them to avoid their presence. The conduct of some of these agents was so bad that even the Indians, who were not strict in their morals, were scandalized. When we take into consideration these circumstances, and the meagreness of the resources of the order, and the difficulties they had in acquiring the language, we can form a faint idea of the hardness of their lot, and it was not without just cause that they decided to send Father d'Olbeau to France with Champlain, in order that the true state of affairs might be urged still further before the king.

Father Le Clercq says: "Meanwhile Monsieur de Champlain employed all his address and prudence, and the intrigues of his friends to obtain what was necessary for the establishment of his new colony. Father d'Olbeau, on his side, spared nothing; both spoke frequently to the members of the company, but in vain, for these people, who always had their ears open to flattering tales of the great profit to be made in the Indian trade, closed them to the requests and entreaties made them. They therefore contented themselves with what they could get."

Father d'Olbeau at length received some consolation and compensation for all his labours, when a bull was issued by the pope, granting a jubilee to New France, which was celebrated at Quebec on July 29th, 1618, and was the first of its kind. For the celebration of this religious festival, the Récollets

A DIFFICULT QUESTION

had built some huts, which were used as stations, and French and Indians proceeded from one of those improvised chapels to the other, singing the psalms and hymns of the church. In the year 1618, the Récollets in New France were only three in number: Fathers Le Caron and d'Olbeau, and Friar Modeste Guines.

During the winter of 1617-18 the missionaries were called upon to decide a difficult question. Two Frenchmen had disappeared in 1616, and the discovery of their bones proved that they had been murdered. A diligent search was instituted which led to the detection of the murderer, who acknowledged his crime. The question of punishment, however, was difficult from the fact that a clerk named Beauchesne, who had been invested with extensive civil power by Champlain, was in the habit of receiving gifts from the Indians. It was consequently considered dangerous to do anything that would displease the Indians, as they were known to be terrible in their vengeance. The Récollets had strongly protested against this method of receiving gifts, which placed the settlement in a false position towards the Indians. It was finally decided to release the prisoner and to accept as hostages two young Indians. When the matter was brought before Champlain, he approved of the course adopted, and stated that it was not a wise policy to be too severe.

This affair, which at one time appeared likely to

CHAMPLAIN

produce disagreeable consequences, passed over without event, and some time after a party of Indians visited Quebec for the purpose of effecting a complete reconciliation. Thus, when Champlain left for France in 1618, the colony was secure.

Father Huet, who accompanied Champlain, was charged with many important missions, one of which related to the administration of baptism to the Indians. They were quite willing to be baptized, but they had no idea of the nature of the sacrament, and although they promised to keep their vows before the ceremony, they soon returned to their old superstitions. Their want of sincerity was a trial to Father Huet, and he desired to have the opinion of the Doctors of the Sorbonne to guide him in his future actions.

During the winter Father Le Caron went to Tadousac in order to continue the work of Father d'Olbeau, and he remained there until the middle of July, 1619. In the interval he had built a residence upon the ground donated by the merchants, and had the satisfaction of leaving one hundred and forty neophytes as the result of the labours of the mission. Father d'Olbeau had his residence at Quebec.

On his return to Canada Father Huet was accompanied by Father Guillaume Poullain, three friars and two labourers. Champlain did not return this year. The Récollets had received authority to build a convent at Quebec, and the Prince de

A RÉCOLLET CONVENT

Condé had contributed fifteen hundred livres towards the object. Charles de Boues, vicar-general of Pontoise, had also made a personal subscription, and accepted the protectorate of the convent, together with the title of syndic of Canadian missions. Other piously disposed persons had also contributed towards the maintenance of the religious institution.

The establishment of a convent in Canada was a ray of light amid the gloom which had hung over the settlement of New France during the past four years, but the rejoicing on this occasion was soon turned into mourning by the unexpected death of Friar du Plessis, who died at Three Rivers on August 23rd, 1619. There were two other deaths during this year which cast a shadow on the colony, that of Anne Hébert, and of her husband, Étienne Jonquest, who survived his wife only a few weeks.

The mission at Three Rivers was placed under the charge of Father Le Caron, and from this date it was the object of the most pastoral solicitude of the Récollets.

CHAPTER VII

THE FUR TRADE

THE earliest reference by Champlain to the fur trade in Canada, is contained in his relation of his voyage to Tadousac in the year 1603. During this journey he encountered a number of Indians in a canoe, near Hare Island, among whom was an Algonquin who appeared to be well versed in the geography of the country watered by the Great Lakes. As a proof of his knowledge, he gave to Champlain a description of the rapids of the St. Lawrence, of Niagara Falls and Lake Ontario. When questioned as to the natural resources of the country, he stated that he was acquainted with a people called the good Iroquois (Hurons) who were accustomed to exchange their peltry for the goods which the French had given to the Algonquins. We have in this statement proof that the French were known to the inhabitants of New France before the year 1603.

In the year 1608, trading was conducted with the Indians at Tadousac, but in 1610 it was alternately at Tadousac, and near Cape de la Victoire at the entrance of the Richelieu River. During the years 1610-11, the fur trade was a failure, although the vessels annually carried from twelve to fifteen

CHAMPLAIN

thousand skins to France, which were sold at one pistole each. From the year 1610, Tadousac ceased to be the rendezvous of traders, and the great centre was at Sault St. Louis, until the year 1618. From this time, for several consecutive years, Three Rivers was the principal trading-post, and finally the Indians went down to Quebec, or to Cape de la Victoire, or du Massacre, and at a still later period the Isle of Richelieu, opposite the parish of Deschambault, some fifteen leagues above Quebec, was chosen as a trading-place.

Champlain was not opposed to the fur trade; on the contrary, he favoured it, provided that it was conducted honestly, as it afforded him opportunities for making new discoveries, and also for maintaining friendly relationship with the Indians. The Récollets had no connection with the trade, although through their efforts commercial intercourse was often facilitated.

Speaking of the trading of 1618, Champlain mentions a class of men who eventually attained considerable influence in colonial affairs. These men were the factors or clerks employed and paid by the merchants. Some of them obtained notoriety on account of their treason and bad conduct, while others were distinguished by their devotedness to Champlain and the missionaries. The clerks or factors were engaged by the fur trading merchants who had their principal factory at Quebec. The staff consisted of a chief clerk, of clerks and underclerks;

DUTIES OF THE FACTORS

and their functions were to receive merchandise on its arrival, to place it in the store, and when the trading was complete, to exchange the goods for skins, which were then carefully packed for exportation. The clerks visited the places chosen by the Indians for trading, and generally conducted the exchanges themselves. Some of them employed the services of interpreters who were readily found, and were frequently sent among the natives to induce them to visit the clerks. The duties of the clerks were not always easily performed. They had many difficulties to encounter, but as successful trading might lead to future promotion, there were advantages connected with the office. Thierry-Desdames, one of the underclerks at Quebec in 1622, was appointed captain of the Island of Miscou, in recognition of his faithful service. This is not the only instance of promotion recorded by Champlain. Beauchesne and Loquin are also mentioned in the Relations of 1618 and 1619.

When Champlain returned from France in 1620, he was accompanied by Jean Baptiste Guers, the business representative of the Duke of Montmorency, who rendered good service to Champlain and the settlers. In the same year Pont-Gravé traded at Three Rivers, and he was assisted by two clerks called Loquin and Caumont, and an underclerk, Roumier. Before leaving for France, Pont-Gravé placed Caumont in charge of his factory. Roumier also left for France, under the pretext that the company refused to increase his wages. The departure of a clerk, however, was of small importance, when we consider the trouble which had arisen among the associates.

In the year 1612, Champlain, it appears, had placed too much confidence in the influence of Henri de Condé, viceroy of New France. This nobleman proved to be a source of trouble rather than a friend to the new colony. Two years after, Champlain formed an association of the merchants of St. Malo and Rouen, who invested their capital for the development of trade in Canada. The chief members of the company were François Porrée, Lucas Legendre, Louis Vermeulle, Mathieu d'Insterlo, Pierre Eon, Thomas Cochon, Pierre Trublet, Vincent Gravé, Daniel Boyer and Corneille de Bellois. By its constitution the operations of the company were to extend over a period of eleven years, and its members engaged to maintain the habitation of Quebec, and a fort, and to build new forts if necessary, and also to pay the expenses of missionaries, and to send labourers and workmen to Canada. The Prince de Condé received a salary of three thousand livres, and the payment of this large amount annually to the viceroy, caused the merchants to neglect their obligations towards Champlain, who was to be Condé's lieutenant in New France.

In the meantime Condé conspired against the Queen Regent and was incarcerated, and the Maréchal de Thémines was temporarily appointed in his

A DARK OUTLOOK

place. The office of secretary to the viceroy would appear to have been lucrative, for one applicant, probably Boyer, offered Thémines four thousand five hundred livres, if he would appoint him to the position. Condé protested against the change which had been made against his agreement, and asked for his salary. De Villemenon, intendant of the admiralty, opposed the application, and claimed the amount of the salary for the Quebec settlement.

While Champlain was in France in 1617 he was told of a proscription from the court of parliament of Paris, ordering him to resign his office of lieutenant of the viceroy, as the Company of Rouen had decided to suppress the salary of the viceroy. Champlain did not take any notice of this injunction, but started for Quebec. On his return to France during the same year (1617) Champlain met the Maréchal de Thémines, in order to induce him, in his capacity of viceroy, to take some interest in the affairs of New France, as the situation there was becoming insupportable. The great personages were quarrelling over money matters; the Estate of Brittany were renewing their demands for freedom of trade, and the merchants were refusing to invest new capital. Champlain had a series of difficulties, which he endeavoured to remove before his return to Quebec, and he drew up his proposals in two large memorials, one of which was presented to the king, and the other to the Chamber of Commerce of Paris.

CHAMPLAIN

In the memorial to the king Champlain explained that France would derive benefit from the colonization of Canada, provided workmen and labourers were sent to the country. He also set forth the necessity of improving the defense of the colony, as an attack might be expected at any time from the English or Dutch. Champlain pointed out to the king, at the same time, that by developing New France, he would be propagating the Catholic faith amongst infidels, and that he would add to his wealth by reason of the revenue to be derived from the vast forests of Canada. He also made known to the king some of the projects which he had in view. Amongst these were certain buildings and works which he proposed to carry out. Quebec was to be named *Ludovica*, in honour of the king. A church was to be erected and dedicated under the title of *Redeemer*, and a fort was to be constructed on the cape of Quebec, flanked with four bastions, which would command the river St. Lawrence. A second fort was to be built opposite Quebec, which would complete the defense of the face of the town, and a third fort would be constructed at Tadousac on a promontory naturally fortified, to be manned by a garrison which would be relieved every six months.

These arrangements would provide for the defense of the country. Champlain also intended to look after the education and the spiritual wants of the settlement, by sending fifteen friars of the

FACTUM TO THE BOARD OF TRADE

Récollet order to New France, who were to found a convent near the Church of the Redeemer. The king was also asked to send three hundred families to the colony, each composed of a husband and wife and two children or a servant under twenty years of age. With these provisions Champlian believed that a settlement might be established in the name of France, which would remain loyal to her interests, since it would rest upon the sure foundation of strength, justice, commerce, and agriculture.

In his explanations to the Chamber of Commerce Champlain dwelt upon the advantages which were to to be derived from fishing, from the lumber industry, agriculture and cattle raising, and from the working of the mines and from trading. In short he endeavoured to induce the associates to continue their operations. The members, however, were under the impression that colonization would place obstacles in the way of commerce, and that the inhabitants would soon monopolize the trade. Some of the associates who were Protestants objected to colonization under Catholic influence, and understanding that Champlain was a staunch Catholic, they decided to have Pont-Gravé appointed as lieutenant of the viceroy, in his place.

Champlain was much affected on finding that he had a rival in Pont-Gravé whom he had always respected as a father, neither would he accept such a humiliating position. The king, however, intervened at this time, and wrote a letter to the associates, requesting them to aid Champlain.

"BY THE KING.

"DEAR AND WELL-BELOVED:—On the report made to us that there has hitherto been bad management in the establishment of the families and workmen sent to the settlement of Quebec, and other places of New France, we write to you this letter, to declare to you our desire that all things should proceed better in future; and to tell you that it will give us pleasure that you should assist, as much as you conveniently can, the Sieur Champlain in the things requisite and necessary for the execution of the commands which he has received from us, to choose experienced and trusty men to be employed in the discovery, inhabiting, cultivating, and sowing the lands; and do all the works which he shall judge necessary for the establishment of the colonies which we desire to plant in the said country, for the good of the service and the use of our subjects; without, however, on account of the said discoveries and settlements, your factors, clerks, and agents in the traffic of peltry, being troubled or hindered in any way whatever during the term which we have granted you. And fail not in this, for such is our pleasure. Given at Paris March 12th, 1618. (Signed) "LOUIS."
  (And below) "POTIER."

The merchants brought their affairs before the

PROVISIONS FOR SETTLERS

notice of the Council of Tours, who decided that Champlain should retain his position. The action of the council was a victory for Champlain, but it was soon followed by another still more agreeable. The associates promised to provide for the organization of emigration during the following year on a scale which would assure the success of the settlement. By this arrangement eighty persons, including three Récollet fathers, would arrive in New France during the year 1619. In order to have the proceedings regularly conducted, Champlain caused papers to be prepared by notaries, which were signed on December 21st, 1618, by Pierre du Gua and Lucas Legendre in the name of the associates, and also by Vermeulle, Corneille de Bellois and Mathieu d'Insterlo. The document is as follows:

"List of persons to be sent to, and supported at, the settlement of Quebec for the year 1619.

"There shall be eighty persons, including the chief, three Récollet fathers, clerks, officers, workmen and labourers. Every two persons shall have a mattress, a paillasse, two blankets, three pairs of new sheets, two coats each, six shirts, four pairs of shoes, and one capote.

"For the arms:—Forty musquets, with their bandoliers, twenty-four pikes, four arquebuses à rouet [wheel-lock] of four to five feet, one thousand pounds of fine powder, one thousand pounds of powder for cannon, one thousand pounds of balls, six thousand pounds of lead, and a match-stump.

CHAMPLAIN

"For the men:—A dozen scythes with their handles, hammers, and other tools; twelve reaping-hooks, twenty-four spades, twelve picks, four thousand pounds of iron, two barrels of steel, ten tons of lime (none having been then found in this country), ten thousand curved, or twenty thousand flat tiles, ten thousand bricks to build an oven and chimneys, two mill-stones (the kind of stone fit for that purpose was not discovered till some years afterwards).

"For the service of the table of the chief:—Thirty-six dishes, as many bowls and plates, six saltcellars, six ewers, two basins, six pots of six pints each, six pints, six chopines (about half a pint) six demy-septiers, the whole of pewter, two dozen table-cloths, twenty-four dozen napkins.

"For the kitchen:—A dozen of copper boilers, six pairs andirons, six frying-pans, six gridirons.

"Shall also be taken out:—Two bulls of one year old, heifers, and as many sheep as convenient; all kinds of seed for sowing.

"The commander of the settlement shall have charge of the arms and ammunition which are actually there, and of those which shall afterwards be sent, so long as he shall be in command; and the clerk or factor who shall reside there shall take charge of all merchandise; as well as of the furniture and utensils of the company, and shall send a regular account of them, signed by him, by the ships.

"Also shall be sent, a dozen mattresses complete, like those of families, which shall be kept in the

THE DUKE OF MONTMORENCY

magazine for the use of the sick and wounded, etc., etc.

"Signed at Paris, December 21st, 1618, and compared with the original [on paper] by the undersigned."

Champlain submitted this document to the king, who approved it, but nevertheless the associates were afterwards unwilling to fulfil its conditions The Prince de Condé having been discharged from prison on October 20th, 1619, the king restored to him his commission of viceroy, and the Company of Rouen granted him a thousand crowns.

The prince gave five hundred crowns to the Récollets for the construction of a seminary at Quebec, and this was his only gift to the settlement of New France. The prince afterwards sold his commission as viceroy to the Duke of Montmorency, Admiral of France, for the sum of eleven thousand crowns. Dolu, grand almoner of the kingdom, was appointed intendant. The duke renewed Champlain's commission as lieutenant of the viceroy, and at the same time advised him to return to Quebec to strengthen his positions everywhere, in order that the country might be secure against invasion.

The patronage of Montmorency greatly encouraged Champlain, for the duke exercised great power. He therefore resolved to take his young wife to Quebec with him, for she had never been to Canada. Champlain concluded his private business

CHAMPLAIN

in France, and took all his effects to the new settlement, as he had determined to take up his residence there. Before leaving France, all the difficulties in connection with his command were removed, and the king wrote him a very gracious letter, in which His Majesty expressed his esteem for his loyal and faithful subject.

The change of viceroy soon brought a further change. Dolu made inquiry into the affairs of the Rouen company, and finding how they had neglected their obligation to take out colonists for New France, recommended to the Duke of Montmorency that the monopoly should be taken from them. This was decided upon, and a new company was organized under the management of two brothers Caën, merchants of Rouen. The new company received the monopoly of trade for eleven years on practically the same conditions as their predecessors (articles of date November 26th, 1620). Time was to show that the Caën company would be no more zealous to fulfill their obligations than their predecessors. But for the moment matters looked more hopeful. Champlain remained in ignorance of this change until the arrival of the vessels in the spring of 1621, when he received letters from M. de Puiseux, *secrétaire des commandements du roi*, from the intendant Dolu, from de Villemenon, intendant of the admiralty, from Guillaume de Caën, the head of the new association, and from the viceroy. The last is here given:—

LETTERS FROM HEADQUARTERS

"MONSIEUR CHAMPLAIN: For several reasons I have thought fit to exclude the former Company of Rouen and St. Malo from the trade with New France, and to assist you and provide you with everything necessary, I have chosen the Sieurs de Caën, uncle and nephew, and their associates: one is a good merchant, and the other a good sea captain, who can aid you well, and make the authority of the king respected in my government. I recommend you to assist him and those who shall apply to you on his part, so as to maintain them in the enjoyment of the privileges which I have granted them. I have charged the Sieur Dolu, intendant of the affairs of the country, to send you a copy of the treaty by the first voyage, so that you may know to what they are bound, in order that they may execute their engagement, as, on my part, I desire to perform what I have promised.

"I have taken care to preserve your appointments, as I believe you will continue to serve the king well.

"Your most affectionate and perfect friend,
"MONTMORENCY.
"From Paris, February 2nd, 1621."

The letter of Louis XIII was also satisfactory:

"CHAMPLAIN: I have perceived by your letters: of August 15th, with what affection you work at your establishment, and for all that regards the good of my service: for which, as I am thankful to you, so I shall have pleasure in recognizing it to your advantage whenever the occasion shall offer: and I have willingly granted some munitions of war, which were required to give you better means to subsist and to continue in that good duty, which I promise myself from your care and fidelity."

"Paris, February 24th, 1621.   Louis."
It was in this manner that the sentence of death was given to the old company.

Several members of the old Company of Rouen and St. Malo were incorporated in the Company of Montmorency, which was composed of Guillaume de Caën, Ezechiel de Caën, Guillaume Robin, three merchants of Rouen; François de Troyes, president of the treasury of France at Orleans; Jacques de Troyes, merchant; Claude Le Ragois, receiver-general of finance at Limoges; Arnould de Nouveau; Pierre de Verton, councillor, and secretary of the king; and François Hervé, merchant of Paris. The two brothers de Caën belonged to the reformed religion.

Dolu advised Champlain to restrain the hands of the clerks of the old company, and to seize all the merchandise in the magazine. He claimed that although this measure was rigorous, it was justified by the fact that the company had not fulfilled its obligations towards the settlement of New France. De Villemenon's letter was dictated in much the same terms. Guillaume de Caën gave notice that he would soon arrive in Quebec with arms and stores for the settlement. Dolu's letter regarding the sei-

DISPUTES OF THE COMPANIES

zure of merchandise was couched in terms that might be considered imperative, nevertheless Champlain deemed it prudent to act with caution, and he therefore conferred with Father George Le Baillif, Guers and Captain Dumay[1] on the subject.

The old company had some clerks at Quebec, who after hearing of the contents of Dolu's letter, were prepared to resist any curtailment of their rights. Champlain appeesed them, and assured them that they would be allowed freedom of trading at least until the arrival of Guillaume de Caën, the extent of whose authority was not yet known.

Caumont, the chief clerk, declared that he was satisfied with this arrangement, but nevertheless the situation was difficult. If the king had given the order to confiscate the merchandise, then Dumay, whose visit to Canada was for the purpose of fur trading, would become the king of commerce in New France, and therefore he had nothing to lose in awaiting de Caën's arrival. He proceeded at once to Tadousac, but instead of meeting de Caën, he found that Pont-Gravé had arrived as the representative of the old company, and that he had with him seventy-five men and some clerks.

Champlain was much distressed on receiving

[1] His correct name was Dumé *dit* Leroy. He made a single voyage to Quebec, and he had on board Jean Baptiste Guers, delegate of the Duke of Montmorency. Dumé was born at St. Gomer de Fly, Beauvais. A member of his family, who resided at Havre de Grâce, was one of the chief consignees of the company of St. Christophe in the West Indies.

CHAMPLAIN

these tidings, for he foresaw a conflict which would possibly entail bloodshed. The clerks also were despondent. In order to avoid a quarrel, Champlain deemed it advisable to protect his men, and he therefore installed his brother-in-law, Eustache Boullé, and Captain Dumay with sixteen men, in the small fort which he had erected at Cape Diamond during the preceding year. Champlain defended himself within the habitation, where he quartered all the men he could dispose of. If the clerks were inclined to fight he would defend his position, but he hoped that these precautionary measures would prove the means of preventing bloodshed.

On June 7th, 1621, three of the clerks of the old company arrived from Tadousac and took up their quarters near the habitation. Father Le Baillif and Jean Baptiste Guers asked them to produce their papers. They declared that they had authority to trade from the old Company of Rouen, which still existed through articles agreed to by the Duke of Montmorency, and that a trial was at present pending between the two societies. On receiving this information from Father Le Baillif, Champlain decided to allow five clerks the necessary merchandise for trading; they were, however, told that the old company had been dissolved, and that the new company only was invested with authority to trade. The clerks were satisfied with Champlain's decision, but they objected to the presence of armed

AN ORDER-IN-COUNCIL

soldiers in the fort, which they claimed was not in accordance with the king's commands. The clerks finally went to Three Rivers to carry on their trade.

On June 13th, Pont-Gravé arrived at Quebec. Here he was questioned as to his authority, although he was treated with the respect and courtesy due to his age and character. Pont-Gravé assured Champlain that the disputes between the two companies would be resolved in a friendly way, and that he had received news to this effect before he sailed from Honfleur. He then started for Three Rivers to join his clerks.

A month after these events, a clerk named Roumier, in the employ of de Caën, arrived with letters from Dolu, de Villemenon, and Guillaume de Caën, and left a copy of an order-in-council in favour of the old company. Champlain also received a letter from the king. The order-in-council granted permission to both companies to trade during the year 1621, provided that both should contribute equally towards the maintenance of the captains, soldiers, and the inhabitants of Quebec.

Foreseeing a conflict between de Caën and Pont-Gravé, Champlain went to Tadousac, and advised de Caën to respect Pont-Gravé's authority. De Caën replied that he could not do so, as he had received authority privately from the king. Champlain therefore assumed the command of Pont-Gravé's vessel, in order to protect his old friend, and thus it happened that this affair which threatened to produce serious consequences, was smoothed over through Champlain's intervention. Pont-Gravé then took possession of his vessel in the presence of de Caën, who offered no opposition, and a few days after they both returned to France.

De Caën had promised to send twenty-five men to Quebec, but he sent only eighteen. A certain quantity of stores was also brought to Quebec at this time by Jacques Halard, and a number of halberds, arquebuses, lances, and many barrels of powder, which were delivered in the presence of Jean Baptiste Varin, who had been sent by Guillaume de Caën, and J. B. Guers.

Father Georges Le Baillif also left for France during the autumn, as a delegate from the inhabitants of the settlement, who had prepared a memorandum of their grievances. This document was signed by Champlain, Father Jamet, Father Le Caron, Louis Hébert, Guillaume Couillard, Eustache Boullé, Pierre Reye, Olivier Le Tardif, J. Groux, Pierre Desportes, Nicholas and J. B. Guers. On his arrival in France, Father Le Baillif had an interview with the king, and placed the memorandum in question in His Majesty's hands. The king admitted that the complaints were well founded, but at the same time he stated that it was impossible to grant all that was requested. The Huguenots were to retain their commercial liberty, and Champlain obtained some supplies, and his salary,

THE NEW COMPANY ESTABLISHED

which was formerly six hundred livres, was increased to twelve hundred.

Father Le Baillif's mission was unfruitful, for he brought word of the amalgamation of the two companies, whose chiefs were Guillaume de Caën, Ezechiel de Caën, and their nephew, Emery de Caën. The order-in-council establishing this large company granted to them the liberty of trading in New France, and all French subjects were eligible for admission to the society. By this arrangement the de Caëns were obliged to pay the sum of ten thousand livres to the members of the old Rouen association, and a sum equal to the value of their goods, barques and canoes. The old company received five-twelfths of the Company of Montmorency, one-twelfth of which was reserved by de Monts, who was at that time living at his residence in Saintonge. By this latter arrangement, however, the de Caëns were relieved from the payment of the ten thousand livres imposed upon them by the order-in-council. When Father Le Baillif returned to Quebec in the spring of 1622, all the old rivalry had disappeared. The Company of Rouen had adopted the name of the Company of Montmorency with the de Caëns as chiefs.

The principal articles stipulated in the agreement were:—

1. Champlain to be lieutenant of the viceroy, with precedence on land, and to command the habitation of Quebec, and to have command of all the

CHAMPLAIN

French residents in New France. Ten men were also to be placed at his disposal, who were to be maintained at the expense of de Caën, who was also to pay to each an annual sum of twenty livres.

2. The company was also to maintain six Récollet fathers, two of whom were to be engaged in missions to the savages.

3. The company was to support and maintain six families of labourers, carpenters and masons, during the period of the agreement, the families to be changed every two years.

4. The company was to pay the sum of twelve hundred francs as a salary to Champlain.

5. Champlain was to enjoy the privilege of trading for eleven years, and to this term the king added another eleven years.

The first man to bring the news of a change of authority was a clerk named Santein, but it was confirmed some days after by the arrival of Pont-Gravé and Guillaume de Caën, who were accompanied by a clerk named Le Sire, an underclerk named Thierry-Desdames,[1] and Raymond de la Ralde. De Caën handed to Champlain a letter from the king, who advised him to recognize the authority of the new company, and also to endeavour to maintain peace and harmony. When de Caën had

---

[1] Thierry-Desdames arrived at Quebec in 1622, as underclerk of the company, which position he occupied until 1628. We lose trace of him after that date, but we find him again in 1639 at Miscou Island, where he served as captain. He was a good Catholic, charitable, and a friend of the Jesuits.

FIRST CANADIAN LAWS

completed his trading at Three Rivers he sailed again for France, leaving Pont-Gravé as chief clerk at Quebec, and Le Baillif as underclerk at Tadousac.

In order to establish good order throughout the country, Champlain published certain ordinances, which should be regarded as the first code of Canadian laws. Although it was desirable to maintain peace, it was also necessary to prepare to resist the attacks of the Iroquois, who were becoming more and more active. A party of the Iroquois had approached Quebec, and were observed to be rambling in the vicinity of the Récollets' convent, on the north shore of the River St. Charles. They finally made an attack, but they were repulsed with loss by the French and the Montagnais, whose chief was Mahicanaticouche, Champlain's friend. This chief was the son of the famous Anadabijou, who had contracted the first alliance with the French at Tadousac in 1603.

In the year 1623, the vessels arrived from France later than usual, and the rendezvous took place at Cape de la Victoire on July 23rd. On this occasion the following persons were present: Champlain, Pont-Gravé, Guillaume de Caën, Captain Duchesne, des Marets, De Vernet, Étienne Brûlé, an interpreter, Loquin, a clerk, Father Nicholas Viel, and Brother Sagard-Théodat.

On his return to Quebec, Champlain declared that certain sailors had appropriated a number of

CHAMPLAIN

beaver skins, and he therefore confiscated them and had them placed in the store, pending the decision of the company. This infraction of the rules of commerce was trifling when compared with the contraband which was carried on freely in the lower St. Lawrence. The merchants of La Rochelle and the Basques were the most notorious in this respect. Their vessels were constantly sailing from one shore to another, trading furs, although they had no authority to do so. They were found at Tadousac, at Bic, and at Green Island. The Spanish, English and Dutch vessels also carried on an illegitimate trade in the same waters. Champlain mentions the fact that a Spanish captain, whose vessel was anchored at Green Island, had sent his sailors at night to Tadousac, in order that they might watch what was being done, and hear what was being said on board the *Admiral.*

At the commencement of the spring of 1624, a dark cloud hung over New France. The winter had been severe, and provisions were scarce. Champlain had only four barrels of flour in the store, so that he was anxiously awaiting assistance. On June 2nd he received good news. A vessel of sixty tons was anchored at Tadousac, laden with pease, biscuits and cider. To the starving settlement this was most welcome, and some days after Guillaume de Caën arrived with still more provisions.

After having traded at Three Rivers, de Caën visited Quebec, the Island of Orleans, and the

TO FRANCE AGAIN

vicinity of Cape Tourmente and the neighbouring islands. He was now the proprietor of these lands, having received them as a gift from the Duke of Montmorency.

Champlain now resolved to recross the ocean, and to take with him his young wife, who had spent four years in Quebec. Emery de Caën was given the command of the settlement in the absence of Champlain. On August 21st two ships sailed from Tadousac, having on board Champlain, Hélène Boullé, Pont-Gravé, Guillaume de Caën, Father Piat, Brother Sagard, J. B. Guers, Joubert, and Captain de la Vigne. At Gaspé, Raymond de la Ralde and a pilot named Cananée joined the party. The voyage was brief and pleasant to Champlain's party, but Cananée's ship was captured by the Turks, and its commander was put to a cruel death.[1]

[1] Cananée was one of the most famous French navigators of his time. From 1608 to 1624 he used to fish on the banks of Miscou and in the gulf. He was at first captain and co-proprietor of the *Mouton*, a vessel of one hundred and twenty tons, but some years later, he commanded the *Ste. Madeleine*, a ship of fifty tons. It was this vessel that the Turks captured on the coast of Bretagne. Cananée was a fervent Catholic.

CHAPTER VIII

CHAMPLAIN, THE JESUITS AND THE SAVAGES

THE first inhabitants of the settlement of New France were the interpreters, clerks, and workmen, employed by the merchants. They were termed the winterers, in opposition to the captains and sailors who visited the colony for the purpose of trading only. The interpreters present an interesting feature in the life of the new colony. Their functions rendered it necessary for them to reside for an indefinite period with an Indian tribe, in order to qualify themselves to act as interpreters for their countrymen during trade, or for the missionaries while catechising or providing other religious exercises. A daily intercourse with the Indians was absolutely essential in order to induce them to keep their appointments with the traders at the established rendezvous. The interpreters had seldom any other occupation, although some of them acted as clerks, and thereby received a larger salary, in addition to a certain number of beaver skins which they could exchange for goods.

Étienne Brûlé and Nicholas Marsolet, who arrived at Quebec with Champlain in the year 1608, acted as interpreters, but at first they did not meet with much success. They were, however, both young

CHAMPLAIN

and intelligent, and Brûlé soon acquired a knowledge of the Huron language, while Marsolet mastered the idiom of the Algonquin tongue. Brûlé spent nearly all his life among the Hurons, who adopted him as a member of their family, while Marsolet accompanied the Algonquins to Allumette Island, and became one of their best friends. Historians of Canada mention the names of many other interpreters of this period, some of whom founded families, while others afterwards returned to France. In the year 1613 three interpreters arrived, Nicholas du Vignau, Jacques Hertel, and Thomas Godefroy. In the year 1618 there was only one arrival, Jean Manet, who took up his residence among the people residing on the shores of Lake Nipissing.

In the year 1619 Jean Nicolet came to Canada, and won great esteem in the country of his choice. He was the father of a large family, the descendants of whom are very numerous. Three more interpreters came in 1621, Du Vernet, Le Baillif, and Olivier Le Tardif, and two in 1623, namely, Jean-Paul Godefroy and Jacques Couillard, and finally in 1624 Jean Richer and Lamontagne, thus making twelve interpreters between the years 1608 and 1625. Of this number the two Godefroys, Marsolet, Nicolet, Hertel, and Le Tardif were distinguished on account of the part which they took in Canadian affairs; and the knowledge which they had obtained of the native languages rendered them competent to

NEW FAMILIES

discuss delicate questions relating to the welfare of the colony. Their services to the authorities, both civil and religious, were therefore at certain periods exceedingly valuable.

It is among the second class of settlers, or winterers, as they were termed that we may fittingly seek for the founders of the Canadian race. From the year 1608 to 1613 not a single settler or head of a family came to Canada, but at this latter date we find the names of Abraham Martin, Nicholas Pivert and Pierre Desportes. They were married and brought their wives and families with them. Abraham Martin and Pierre Desportes had each a daughter, and Pivert had a niece. Guillaume Couillard arrived during the same year, but he was a bachelor. We have already spoken in a previous chapter of the return of Champlain from France in the year 1617, on which occasion he was accompanied by Louis Hébert and his family. There also arrived in 1617, Étienne Jonquest, to whom we have likewise referred. In 1618 another family took up its residence in New France, namely Adrien Duchesne, surgeon, and his wife. Eustache Boullé, brother-in-law to Champlain, came over in 1618, and two families arrived in 1619, but they were immediately sent back, as the occupation of the head of one of the families was that of a butcher, and the other was a needle manufacturer, and there was no opening for either in a new settlement. In the year 1620,

CHAMPLAIN

the settlers gave a cordial welcome to Hélène Boullé, who was attended by three female servants. From the year 1620 to 1625, history is silent as to new arrivals. Champlain had made every effort to induce settlers to take up their residence in Quebec, but the population was still very scanty.

There were really only seven settled families at this time, composed of twenty persons, seven men and seven women, and six children. Their names were as follows:—Abraham Martin and his wife Marguerite Langlois, and his two daughters, Anne and Marguerite; Pierre Desportes and his wife Françoise Langlois, and a girl named Hélène; Nicholas Pivert and his wife Marguerite Lesage, and their niece; Louis Hébert and his wife Marie Rollet, and a son named Guillaume; Adrien Duchesne and his wife; Guillaume Couillard, his wife, Guillemette Hébert, and a girl named Louise; Champlain and his wife Hélène Boullé.

When Abraham Martin came to Quebec, he was twenty-four years of age. The official documents refer to him as king's pilot, and the Jesuits named him Maître Abraham, while to the people he was Martin l'Ecossais. His family gave to the Catholic Church of Canada her second priest in chronological order. This priest, who was born at Quebec, was named Charles Amador. After having served as a mariner for the Company of Rouen, Abraham Martin became a farmer, and was the proprietor of two portions of land, consisting of thirty-two

THE PLAINS OF ABRAHAM

acres.[1] He received twenty acres of land from Adrien Duchesne, and twelve acres from the Company of New France, on December 4th, 1635.[2] This property was named the Plains of Abraham, and all the ground in the immediate vicinity gradually assumed the same title. A part of the famous conflict fought on September 13th, 1759, and known as the Battle of the Plains of Abraham, actually occurred on the ground owned by Abraham Martin, and thus it is that the name of this first settler has been perpetuated in prose and verse.

Louis Hébert, the son of a Parisian apothecary, followed the profession of his father in Canada. He first tried to establish himself at Port Royal, where we find him in the year 1606. He left Port Royal in 1607, but he appears to have returned there, as in the year 1613 he is mentioned as acting as lieutenant in the place of Biencourt, son of Poutrincourt. When Port Royal was abandoned, Hébert returned to France, where he met Champlain, who induced him to turn his steps towards Canada once more. Soon after his second visit to New France, he commenced to build a residence in the Upper Town of Quebec, upon the summit of Mountain Hill. This building, which was of stone, measured thirty-eight feet in length, and was nineteen feet broad.

[1] For a plan of Abraham Martin's property, see, *The Story of the Siege and the Battle of the Plains of Abraham*, by A. G. Doughty.

[2] See *Deed of Concession*, p. 414, Trans. R. S. C., 1899, by A. G. Doughty.

CHAMPLAIN

It was in this house that Father Le Jeune said mass when he came to Quebec in 1632. Hébert received some concessions of land from the companies, and at once commenced to cultivate it, so that he was able to live from its produce. Champlain praises him for this course. Hébert died in the year 1627, from mortal injuries caused by a fall. He was buried in the cemetery of the Récollets, at the foot of the great cross, according to his desire.

The Récollet fathers lived until the year 1620 in their humble residence near the chapel and habitation of Quebec, in the Lower Town. In the year 1619 they employed some workmen to fell trees on the shores of the River St. Charles, near an agreeable tract of land which Hébert had cleared. It was situated at half a league from the habitation, and the people of Quebec hoped at that time to build the town there. During the winter each piece of timber was prepared for the building, and the savages assisted in the work. On June 3rd, 1620, the first stone of the convent was solemnly laid by Father d'Olbeau. The arms of the king were engraved upon the stone near those of the Prince de Condé. The convent was finished and blessed on May 25th, 1621, and dedicated to Notre Dame des Anges. It was on this date that the name of St. Charles was given to the river Ste. Croix, or the Cabir-Coubat of the Indians, in honour of the Reverend Charles de Ransay des Boues, syndic of the Canadian missions.

THE RÉCOLLET FATHERS

There were six Récollet fathers at Quebec in 1621, and two brothers. Fathers Guillaume Galleran and Irénée Piat came in 1622, the former in the capacity of visitor and superior. A coincidence of their arrival was the induction of the first religious novitiate. Pierre Langoissieux, of Rouen, took the monastic habit under the name of Brother Charles, at a special ceremony in the presence of Champlain and his wife, and some Frenchmen and Indians. Three young men also received the small scapulary of the Franciscan order. Father Piat left Quebec for the Montagnais mission, while Father Huet was sent to Three Rivers, and Father Poullain to the Nipissing mission in the west. In the year 1623, Father Nicholas Viel and Brother Gabriel Sagard-Théodat, the historian of the Huron mission, arrived. They were entertained at the convent of Notre Dame des Anges. At the solemn Te Deum, which was sung in the chapel on this occasion, there were present seven fathers and four brothers. Fathers Le Caron and Viel, and Brother Sagard arranged for some Indian guides to conduct them to the Huron country, where they arrived on July 23rd. The party spent the winter among the Hurons, and during the following year Brother Sagard was recalled to France by his superiors. The Récollets continued to conduct services in the small chapel in the Lower Town, which served as the parochial church of Quebec.

In the year 1624 the French colony was placed

under the patronage of Saint Joseph, who has remained from that date the patron saint of Canada. Champlain was at this time in France, and had met Montmorency at St. Germain-en-Laye, after the Récollets had complained of the conduct of the Huguenots. While the missionaries were celebrating mass, the Huguenots annoyed them by singing psalms, and they occupied the poop-royal on board the vessels for their services, while the Catholics were compelled to assemble in the forecastle, without distinction of persons. The Récollets also complained of the negligence of the associates, who had not provided for the material requirements of the mission. Father Piat set forth that while the missionaries were prepared to sacrifice their health and their mother country in order to civilize the Indians, they were not ready, under the circumstances, to die simply for the want of food, when it was the duty of the associates to provide for them. Father Piat also suggested the advisability of forming a seminary for young Indians, as a means of developing their moral character, of teaching them the rudiments of religion, and whereby the Récollets might acquire a knowledge of the Indian language. Realizing that they were unable to found such an institution alone, they decided to ask assistance from the Jesuits, who had great influence at court, and who might possibly be able to establish such a building from their own resources. If these resolutions had been known, the

HENRI DE LÉVIS

Huguenots would doubtless have prevented the Jesuits' departure, but the news was only made public when it was too late to formulate any opposition.

Champlain, who was at this time endeavouring to induce the merchants to carry out their engagements, thought it advisable not to take any part in urging the requests of the mission, for fear of compromising its success, and he considered it the best policy to be very discreet. Father Coton, provincial of the Jesuit order, accepted with pleasure the proposals of the Récollets, as the order was always glad of an opportunity of preaching the gospel in distant lands. The Jesuits had already founded the Acadian mission, but its results had much disappointed their hopes. Champlain was pleased to learn that the desire of the Récollets was accomplished, although he had taken no part towards its fulfilment. Indeed his services were fully employed elsewhere. The old merchants were fighting with the new ones, the dispute arising from the different methods of recruiting crews for their ships.

These petty quarrels, which were constantly brought to the notice of Montmorency, caused him much annoyance, and he consequently resigned his position of viceroy in favour of his nephew, Ventadour, peer of France and governor of Languedoc, for a sum of one hundred thousand livres. The king gave his assent to the transaction, and Henri de Lévis, duc de Ventadour, received his commission,

CHAMPLAIN

dated March 25th, 1625. He is described as a pious man, who had no other desire than the glory of God. The duke appointed Champlain as his lieutenant, and ordered him to erect forts in New France wherever he should deem it necessary, and empowered him to create officers of justice to maintain peace and harmony.

Endued with such powers, Champlain did not hesitate to continue his work. The duke's appointment was also received with favour by the Récollets and Jesuits. The associates were not friendly disposed towards the Jesuits, but seeing that they did not ask any assistance from them, they made no opposition to their departure for Canada.

Guillaume de Caën took with him on his vessel three Jesuit fathers and two brothers. These were Fathers Charles Lalemant, Jean de Brébeuf and Enemond Massé. The brothers were François Charton and Gilbert Burel. Father Lalemant, formerly director of the college of Clermont, was appointed director of the mission. Champlain speaks of him as a very devoted and zealous man. Father Massé had been previously in Acadia, where he proved his devotedness to the Indians. Father de Brébeuf, the youngest of the three, was distinguished by reason of his mature judgment and great prudence. The number of the Récollets was increased by the arrival of Father Joseph de la Roche d'Aillon, a man of noble and exalted character.

De Caën's vessel sailed from Dieppe, and although

L'ANTICOTON

the voyage was long, it was a pleasant one. When the Jesuits reached Quebec, they met with strong opposition from the clerks, and there was no residence prepared for them. The only course which appeared open to them was to return to France, unless they could find a lodging with the Récollets.

In the meantime the clerks circulated a pamphlet amongst the families of the settlement, with a view to creating a prejudice against the Jesuits. It was *L'Anticoton*,[1] a libellous communication, which had been proven false by Father Coton. The Récollets at once extended a courteous invitation to the Jesuits, which they gratefully accepted, and took up their residence in the convent. The Récollets also begged them to accept as a loan the timber work of a building which had been prepared for their own use.

The gratitude of the Jesuits under these circumstances, is not sufficiently well known. Father Lale-

[1] Father Mariana, a Jesuit, having published a book entitled, *De Regi et Regis Institutione*, in which he denounced tyranny and its fomenters, the court ordered that the work should be burnt, under the pretext that Ravaillac, who had assassinated Henri IV, had taken advantage of the Jesuit's authority to excuse his murder. It was certain that the Jesuits were the best friends of the late king. Nevertheless, they had to suffer the hostility of a certain part of the secular clergy. Father Coton, a Jesuit, published at once a pamphlet under the title, "Is it lawful to kill the tyrants?" in which he taught that it is not lawful to kill a king, except he abuses his authority. An answer to the pamphlet, published anonymously, soon appeared, which was a satirical paper rather than a refutation of Father Coton's letter. During the same year a new satirical paper against the Jesuits was printed, entitled *L'Anticoton*. It was translated into Latin.

mant's letter addressed to the Provincial of the Récollets in France, admirably sets forth their position, and will be read with interest by every student of this portion of our history.

"REVEREND FATHER: Pax Christi. It would be too ungrateful were I not to write to your Reverence to thank you for the many letters lately written in our favour to the Fathers who are here in New France, and for the charity which we have received from the Fathers, who put us under eternal obligation. I beseech our good God to be the reward of you both. For myself, I write to our Superiors that I feel it so deeply that I will let no occasion pass of showing it, and I beg them, although already most affectionately disposed, to show your whole holy order the same feelings. Father Joseph will tell your Reverence the object of his voyage, for the success of which we shall not cease to offer prayers and sacrifices to God. This time we must advance in good earnest the affairs of our Master, and omit nothing that shall be deemed necessary. I have written to all who, I thought, could aid it, and I am sure they will exert themselves, if affairs in France permit. Your Reverence, I doubt not, is affectionately inclined, and so *virtus unitas*, our united effort, will do much. Awaiting the result, I commend myself to the Holy Sacrifice of your Reverence, whose most humble servant I am.

"CHARLES LALEMANT."
"Quebec, July 28th, 1625."

DE CAËN ACCUSED

The Jesuits accepted the hospitality of the Récollets until the convent which they built on the opposite side of the river St. Charles, was ready for their habitation. It was situated near the entrance of the river Lairet, about two hundred paces from the shore. We shall meet them there a little later, working hard, in common with the Récollets with whom they were good friends, for the civilization of the Indians.

When Guillaume de Cäen returned to France, he was summoned to appear before the tribunal of the state council, as he had not put into effect all the articles of his contract. The chief complaint against him was that the admiral or commodore of the fleet was not a Catholic. For this appointment, however, he was not responsible, as it was made by the associates, and he therefore summoned them to give their explanations before the admiralty judge. The case was finally settled by His Majesty's council in favour of Guillaume de Caën, on the condition that he should at once appoint a Catholic. Raymond de la Ralde was the officer of his choice.

Champlain started at once for Dieppe, together with Eustache Boullé whom he appointed his lieutenant, and Destouches, his second lieutenant. Their departure for Canada occurred on April 24th, 1626, and there were five vessels in the squadron: the *Catherine*, two hundred and fifty tons, commanded

CHAMPLAIN

by de la Ralde;[1] *La Flèque*, two hundred and sixty tons, with Emery de Caën as vice-admiral; *L'Alouette*, eighty tons, and two other vessels, one of two hundred tons, and the other of one hundred and twenty tons.

Champlain was on board the *Catherine*, and he arrived at Percé on June 20th. Before anchoring at Tadousac, Emery de Caën caused his crew to assemble on deck, and he there informed them that the Duc de Ventadour desired that psalms should not be sung, as they had been accustomed to sing them on the Atlantic. Two-thirds of the crew grumbled at this order, and Champlain advised de Caën to allow meetings for prayer only. This ruling was judicious, although it was not accepted with pleasure.

At Moulin Baude, near Tadousac Bay, Champlain received intelligence that Pont-Gravé, who had wintered at Quebec, had been very ill, and that the inhabitants had resolved to leave the country at the earliest opportunity owing to the sufferings which they had endured from famine.

When Champlain arrived at Quebec on July 5th, 1626, he found all the settlers in good health, but

[1] Raymond de la Ralde who was a Catholic, was the first captain of the island of Miscou, the history of which commenced in 1620. Guillaume de Caën appointed de la Ralde as his lieutenant to protect the trade in the Gulf of St. Lawrence against the Basques and others, especially at Percé, Gaspé, and Miscou. From the year 1627, de la Ralde ceased to be of importance, as his fortunes followed the de Caëns.

FORT ST. LOUIS

little had been done towards the building of the fort, or towards repairing the habitation. He, therefore, set twenty men to work at once. Emery de Caën left Quebec in order to carry on trade with the Indians. There were at Quebec at this time fifty-five persons, of whom eighteen were labourers. Champlain wished to have ten men constantly employed at the fort, but Guillaume de Caën had promised them elsewhere, and the merchants obliged them to work at the habitation, which they considered more useful than the fort. Champlain, however, did not agree with them on this point.

The oldest fortification of Quebec was commenced in the year 1620, on the summit of Cape Diamond, and the work was continued in 1621, when Champlain was able to establish a small garrison within the walls. Communication was opened between the habitation and the fort during the winter of 1623-4, by means of a small road, less abrupt than the former one. The fort was named Fort St. Louis.

In April 1624, a strong wind carried away the roof of the fort, and transported it a distance of thirty feet, over the rampart. During this storm the gable of Louis Hébert's residence was also destroyed. This accident caused some delay to the works, and the merchants still maintained their opposition to the construction of the fort. "If we fortify Quebec," they said, "the garrisons will be the masters of the ground, and our trade will be over." Guillaume de Caën supported the opposition by saying that the

CHAMPLAIN

Spaniards would take possession of New France, if a boast were made of its resources. The king, finally, had to undertake the defence of the colony alone.

Before leaving for France in 1624, Champlain had ordered the workmen to gather fascines for the completion of the fort, but upon his return to Canada, two years later, he found that nothing had been done. Champlain therefore decided to demolish the old fort, and to construct a more spacious one with the old materials, composed of fascines, pieces of wood and grass, after the Norman method. The fort was flanked with two bastions of wood and grass, until such time as they could be covered with stone. The fort was ready for habitation at the commencement of the year 1629, and Champlain took up his residence there at this date, with two young Indian girls whom he had adopted as his children. After the capitulation of Quebec in 1629, Louis Kirke resided in the fort with a part of his crew.[1]

Although Champlain was not satisfied with the conduct of the merchants towards the French, he was nevertheless pleased with the Indian tribes. This noble care and management of these poor natives constitute one of the brightest pages of his life. If we wish to form an impartial judgment of the heroic qualities of Champlain, we must study his daily relations with the chiefs of the various

[1] Champlain died within Fort St. Louis, and the Governor Montmagny had the building restored under the title of Château St. Louis, which name it bore until its complete demolition.

RELATIONS WITH THE INDIANS

tribes. It is here that his true character is revealed to us, and we are forced to admire both the patience and care which he bestowed upon these people, and also his exercise of diplomacy which rendered him from the first the most beloved and respected of the French. His word commanded passive obedience, and to maintain his friendship they were willing to make any sacrifice which he desired. In this respect Champlain was more successful than the missionaries, nor is it a matter of surprise that his memory was cherished among the Indians longer than that of Father Le Caron or of Father de Brébeuf. In their appreciation of character, the Indians recognized instinctively that the calling of the missionaries rendered their lives more perfect than that of a man of the world, but the special characteristics and virtues of each did not escape their penetration. Champlain took every care to preserve his friendship with the Indians, not only on his own account, but also for the sake of the traders, and of commerce generally, for his name acted as a safe-conduct. Champlain had another ambition. He realized that if he could induce the Indians to gather in the vicinity of Quebec, they would prove a means of defence against the incursions of enemies. It seems to have been a good policy, and the Jesuits who adopted the same means had reason to be satisfied with their action.

In the year 1622 Champlain tried to establish the Montagnais near Quebec. Miristou, their chief, was willing, and they began to cultivate the land in the

CHAMPLAIN

vicinity of La Canardière, on the north shore of the river St. Charles. By living in the midst of such a community, Champlain hoped to be able to derive new information regarding the country.

The sempiternal question of an open sea, admitting a free passage from Europe to China, was constantly under the consideration of navigators. Whether or not the founder of Quebec believed in this passage, we are not prepared to assert, as he does not make any definite statement, but from his Relations it is evident that he hoped to ascertain whether it were possible to reach the far west by means of the river St. Lawrence and the Great Lakes. He knew that he could serve the interest of the mother country by obtaining new data, and his opinions were well received in France, although the recent wars had somewhat engrossed public attention. The travels of the Récollets in the Huron country had not resulted in the discovery of new territory, and the interpreters had nothing further to do than to discover new tribes with whom trade might be developed. Western Canada had consequently been neglected both for the want of explorers and of resources, as Champlain was of course unable to explore the whole American continent, and at the same time govern the colony of New France, where his presence was required as much as possible.

Champlain tried to effect an alliance with the Iroquois during the year 1622, and for this purpose

A CRIME CONDONED

he sent two Montagnais to their country as delegates. In the meantime a double murder occurred in the colony. A Frenchman named Pillet and his companion were murdered by an unknown party. The facts were brought to the notice of the court in France, and it was decided to pardon the murderer on the condition that he would confess his crime, and publicly ask for pardon. Champlain appears to have been anxious to assert his authority, on this occasion, for the prevention of such crimes, but the merchants were inclined to condone the offence, and one day Guillaume de Caën in the presence of Champlain and some captains, took a sword, and caused it to be cast into the middle of the St. Lawrence, in order that the Indians might understand that the crime even as the sword, was buried forever. The effect of this action was otherwise than desired. The Hurons ridiculed the affair, and said that they had nothing to fear in the future if they murdered a Frenchman.

The murderer was a Montagnais, and the tribe consequently approved of this lack of justice. Champlain, however, desired a more severe imposition of the law. The Montagnais were perhaps the most dangerous of Champlain's allies, especially as their treachery was marked by the outward appearance of serious friendship. In the Montagnais were united all the vices of the other Indian tribes as well as the bad features of some of the Europeans, especially those of the Rochelois and Basques. They

CHAMPLAIN

were bold and independent, but Champlain soon showed them, by ceasing to care for them, that he was not to be imposed upon. Fearing to lose the friendship of Champlain, they endeavoured to regain the position which they had in a measure lost; but instead of remaining passive, they boasted of the ease with which they could find protectors and advocates amongst the French. This conduct did not please Champlain, who would have preferred to find a people more amenable to natural laws, which are in themselves a defence against murder.

The Montagnais who had been sent to the Iroquois returned to Quebec in July, 1624. They had been courteously received, and as a result of their negotiations, a general meeting of the Indians was held at Three Rivers. There might be seen Hurons, Algonquins, Montagnais, Iroquois, and the French with their interpreters. The meeting was conducted with perfect order. There were many speeches, followed by the feast pantagruelic. The war hatchet was buried, so that Champlain could leave for France without being very anxious as to the fate of his compatriots.

The alliance of 1624 did not last long, however, owing to the imprudence of the Montagnais who had journeyed to the Dutch settlement on the banks of the Hudson and promised to assist the settlers in their wars against the Mohicans and Iroquois. Champlain interfered, and reminded the Montagnais that they were bound to observe the treaty of 1624, and

RUMOURS OF WAR

there was no reason to break it. "The Iroquois," said Champlain, "ought to be considered as our friends as long as the war hatchet is not disinterred, and I will go myself to help them in their wars, if necessary."

This language pleased the chief of the Montagnais, and he asked Champlain to send some one to Three Rivers, if he could not go himself, in order to prevent the other nations from fighting against the Iroquois. Eustache Boullé was sent on this delicate mission, but as opinion was divided as to the advisability of the war, it was decided to wait until the arrival of the vessels. Emery de Caën arrived soon after, and hastened to meet the allies, who, according to rumour, were preparing to go to war against the Iroquois. In addition to this a party had gone to Lake Champlain, where they had made two Iroquois prisoners, who were, however, delivered by the murderer of Pillet.

Champlain and Mahicanaticouche arrived in the meantime, whereupon a general council was held. Champlain severely blamed the authors of this escapade, the consequences of which might be terrible. It was resolved to send a new embassy to the Five Nations at once, composed of Cherououny, called *Le Réconcilié* by the French, Chimeourimou, chief of the Montagnais, Pierre Magnan, and an Iroquois, adopted when young by a Montagnais widow. The delegates left for Lake Champlain on July 24th, 1627. One month after, an Indian came to Quebec with

CHAMPLAIN

the news that the four delegates had been murdered by the Tsonnontouans. Magnan had murdered one of his compatriots in France, and by coming to Canada had evaded justice.

This massacre put an end to thoughts of peace. In September some Iroquois were known to be *en route* for Quebec, evidently with hostile motives. It was just at this time that a number of savages were coming from a distance of fifty or sixty leagues to fish in the river St. Lawrence. Nothing serious happened from the visit of the Iroquois, and Champlain was able to visit his habitation at Cape Tourmente without danger. In his absence, however, a double murder was committed at La Canardière. Two Frenchmen, one named Dumoulin, and the other Henri, a servant of the widow Hébert, were found dead, having been shot with muskets.

The murderer's intention had been to kill the baker of the habitation, and a servant of Robert Giffard, the surgeon. Champlain was anxious to punish this murderer, but the difficulty was to discover him. Champlain summoned all the captains of the Montagnais, and having set forth all the favours which he had bestowed upon the nation, contrasted them with the conduct which he had received at their hands since 1616. There had already been four murders of which they were guilty. Champlain therefore demanded that they should find and give up the guilty party. One Montagnais who was suspected, was examined, but he denied everything.

THE MONTAGNAIS

Champlain, however, ordered him to be detained in jail until the real criminal should be found.

During the winter of 1628, about thirty Montagnais, miserable and hungry, came to the habitation, asking for bread. Champlain took this opportunity of pointing out to them the evil of their race, and of the crimes they had committed. They declared that they knew nothing whatever of the crime, and to show that they were not responsible they offered three young girls to Champlain to be educated. Champlain accepted them and treated them as his own children, naming them *Foi, Espérance*, and *Charité*.

After having kept the Montagnais in jail for fourteen months he was released, as there was no proof against him. Champlain learned soon after that he was not guilty, and that the real criminal was dead, being none other than Mahicanaticouche, one of the captains of the Montagnais.

CHAPTER IX

THE COMPANY OF NEW FRANCE OR HUNDRED ASSOCIATES

IN spite of Champlain's strenuous efforts, the permanent existence of New France seemed as yet problematical. At a time when internal peace was imperative the domination of the mercantile companies came to increase the distress of the struggling colony. The difficulties of colonization likewise were immense, and Quebec at the period of which we write, instead of being a thriving town, had scarcely the appearance of a small village. In the year 1627 it could boast only six private residences. The Récollets were living at their convent, but the Jesuits had not completed their new building. The Récollets had abandoned the Huron mission as their numbers were diminishing every year, and they were too poor to continue their ministrations without assistance. They still held in charge the missions at Quebec and at Tadousac. Father d'Olbeau, who had been present at the opening of the Récollet convent at Quebec, saw its doors closed. He remained, however, at his post, and rendered valuable assistance to Champlain.

The Jesuits made great personal efforts for the advancement of the colony, and Father Noyrot had

CHAMPLAIN

sailed for Canada with a number of workmen and a good store of provisions, but unfortunately his vessel did not reach Quebec.

The negligence of Montmorency's company was the principal cause why Quebec was abandoned to its own resources. Champlain was powerless against the ill-will of the company, and the only redress was in the person of the king. Cardinal Richelieu, who was superintendent of the navigation and commerce of France, resolved to reform the remnant of a company founded in 1626, and composed of one hundred associates, for conducting the commerce of the East and West. As the duc de Ventadour had resigned the office of viceroy, the cardinal held a meeting of many rich and zealous persons in his hotel at Paris, whose names would be a guarantee of the success of the colonization of New France, and also of its religious institutions. Among those present were Claude de Roquemont, Sieur de Brison, Louis Houel, Sieur du Petit-Pré, Gabriel de Lattaignant, formerly mayor of Calais, Simon Dablon, syndic of Dieppe, David Duchesne, councillor and alderman of Havre de Grâce, and Jacques Castillon, citizen of Paris.

On April 29th, 1627, the cardinal and these personages signed the act which founded the Company of New France. In the preamble it is mentioned that the colonization in New France shall be Catholic only, as this was regarded as the best means of converting the Indians. The associates pledged

PLEDGES OF THE ASSOCIATES

themselves to send two or three hundred men to New France during the year 1628, and to augment this number to four thousand within fifteen years from this date, i.e., by the year 1643. They agreed to lodge, feed and entertain the settlers for a period of three years, and after that date to grant to each family a tract of land sufficiently prepared for cultivation. Three priests were to be maintained at each habitation, at the expense of the company, for a period of fifteen years.

The king granted to the company numerous privileges, the lands of New France, the river St. Lawrence, islands, mines, fisheries, Florida, together with the power of conceding lands in these countries, and the faculty of granting titles, honours, rights and powers, according to the condition, quality, or merit of the people. His Majesty also granted to the company the monopoly of the fur and leather trade from January 1st, 1628, until December 31st, 1643, reserving for the French people in general the cod and whale fisheries. In order to induce his subjects to settle in New France the king announced that during the next fifteen years all goods coming from the French colony should be free of duty.

This act was signed on April 29th, 1627, and the letters patent ratifying the articles were signed on May 6th, 1628. The letters patent also ratified some other provisions made on May 7th, 1627, namely:—(1.) A capital of three hundred thousand livres, in shares of three thousand livres each.

CHAMPLAIN

(2.) The society to adopt the name of the Compagnie de la Nouvelle France. (3.) The management of the company to be conducted through twelve directors, with full powers to name officers, to distribute lands, establish factors or clerks, to conduct trade and dispose of the joint-stock.

Of these twelve directors six were obliged to live in Paris. The names of the twelve directors who were elected are here given :—Simon Alix, councillor and king's secretary; Pierre Aubert, councillor and king's secretary; Thomas Bonneau, Sieur du Plessis; Pierre Robineau, treasurer of cavalry; Raoul L'Huillier, merchant of Paris; Barthélemy Quentin, merchant of Paris; Jean Tuffet, merchant of Bordeaux; Gabriel Lattaignant, formerly mayor of Calais; Jean Rozée, merchant of Rouen; Simon Lemaistre, merchant of Rouen; Louis Houel, comptroller of saltworks at Brouage; Bonaventure Quentin, Sieur de Richebourg.

These directors were elected for a term of two years, and six of them had to be replaced at each election. The first term of office expired on December 31st, 1629. The election was held in Paris at the house of the intendant, Jean de Lauzon, king's councillor, master of requests and president of the Grand Council. Cardinal Richelieu and the Duke d'Effiat headed the list of the Hundred Associates. We find also the name of Samuel Champlain, captain of the king's marine, of Isaac de Razilly, chevalier de St. Jean de Jérusalem,

OLD DOCUMENTS

Sébastien Cramoisy, the famous printer; François de Ré, Sieur Gand, and many important merchants of Paris, Rouen, Calais, Dieppe, Bordeaux, Lyons, Bayonne, and Havre de Grâce.

This association was formed under auspicious circumstances; its members possessed wealth and influence, and they were certainly in a position to remove the difficulties which had hindered the growth of New France from its foundation.[1]

While these transactions were in progress Champlain was living at Quebec in want of even the necessaries of life. For the past two years Champlain had established a farm for raising cattle at the foot of Cape Tourmente. Some farm buildings and dwellings for the men were erected there, and Champlain visited the place every summer to see that the work was properly carried on. The Récollets had a chapel there in which they said mass from time to time. In 1628 this establishment was in a flourishing condition, and Champlain believed it

[1] All that relates to the formation of the Company of New France is contained in a series of documents entitled, *Edits, Ordonnances royaux*. The first document is entitled, *Compagnie du Canada, establie sous le titre Nouvelle France, par les articles du vingt-neuf auril et sept May, mil six cens vingt-sept*. We find it in the *Mercure François* (t. xiv., part ii., p. 232) and also in the *Mémoires sur les possessions Françoises en Amérique* (t. iii., pp. 3, 4, and 5). This document is double, the first containing twenty articles, and the second thirty-one, which essentially differ. The act of April 29th, 1627, gives the reasons which had engaged the king to establish a new company, its obligations, and the advantages which it will get from Canada. The act of May 7th is the deed of association, which contains the whole organization of the company, its rules, and all that concerns the administration of its

CHAMPLAIN

would ultimately prove of great value to the inhabitants. The colony in the meantime had to rely upon the mother country for provisions, and for flour which could not be produced in Canada.

The new company sent out four vessels in 1628 under the command of Claude de Roquemont, laden with provisions, munitions, and a number of men. This first shipment cost 164,720 livres or about $33,000 of our currency. This large outlay was proof that the associates were determined to maintain the new Canadian settlement. The fleet sailed from Dieppe on May 3rd, and arrived at Percé about the middle of July. During the voyage Roquemont was often exposed to the attacks of the English and Dutch vessels, but he preferred to alter his course rather than to fight. The vessels stopped at the Island of Anticosti, where the crews landed, and planted a cross in token of their gratitude to God, who had protected them.

funds. The validity of the articles of April 29th, 1628, was officially known by an act passed on August 5th, 1628, and the validity of the articles of May 7th took place on August 6th, of the same year. These articles had been confirmed by an order-in-council, on May 6th, 1628, at La Rochelle. On the same day Louis XIII had issued patents confirming the order-in-council. On May 18th Richelieu had ratified the articles of April 29th and of May 7th.

These various documents were published in 1628, one part of them in the *Mercure François*, and the other in a pamphlet, large in quarto of twenty-three pages. The list of the Hundred Associates was also printed in a small pamphlet of eight pages, bearing as title: *Noms, surnoms et Qualitez des Associez En la Compagnie de la Nouvelle France, suyvant les jours et dates de leurs signatures*.

KIRKE'S ATTACK

Some days afterwards they reached Percé, and a little later entered Gaspé Bay. Roquemont was here informed by the savages that five large English vessels were anchored in Tadousac harbour. It was the fleet of David Kirke,[1] who was going to make an assault on Quebec, after having devastated the Acadian coast. Roquemont at once sent Thierry-Desdames to St. Barnabé Island, where he had intended to go himself. Roquemont left Gaspé on July 15th, 1628, and proceeded up the St. Lawrence, hoping that he would be able to escape his powerful enemies, as the French vessels were not properly armed for a regular fight. Unhappily, on the eighteenth the French came within cannon shot of the British fleet. For a period of fourteen hours the vessels cannonaded each other, and over twelve hundred shots were exchanged. The French having exhausted their stock of balls used the lead of their fishing lines instead. Finally Roquemont perceived

[1] About the year 1596 George Kirke, of Norton, county of Derby, married Elizabeth Goudon, of Dieppe, and had issue five boys and two girls. The eldest boy was named David, the second son was Louis; and the third, Thomas; the fourth, John; and the fifth, James. In the year 1629 David was thirty-two years of age, Louis was thirty, and Thomas twenty-six years of age. These are the three heroes of the Quebec assault.

George Kirke was a member of the Company of Adventurers, and he died on December 17th, 1629. In 1637 David received as a concession the New-found-land. After some difficulties which he had to suffer, David Kirke died in the year 1656. His widow claimed the sum of £60,000 for the part that the Kirkes had taken in bringing about the capitulation of Quebec, but the king paid no attention to these claims, and the Kirke family became poor.

that his vessel was sinking, and asked for terms. It was decided that no penalties should be exacted, and that the English admiral should take possession of the ships. The French crews were taken on board the British vessels, which thereupon set sail for England. The British commander soon realized that he had too many persons on board, and some of the families and the Récollet fathers were put off on the Island of St. Pierre. Among the families were a Parisian named Le Faucher, who with his wife and five children were bound for Quebec, Robert Giffard, surgeon, his wife and three girls, and fifteen or sixteen sailors. Kirke left them on this island with some provisions and a small Basque vessel.

The Basques who were hidden in the mountains came down upon the French after the English were out of sight, and threatened to kill them if they attempted to escape in their vessel. They at last allowed the sailors to go elsewhere in consideration of a certain amount of biscuit and cider. They embarked in a frail shallop, and eventually arrived at Plaisance on the coast of Newfoundland, where some French fishermen conducted them to France. The others ultimately reached Spain with the Basques.

Some writers have blamed Roquemont for trying to avoid a fight. His conduct is pardonable, however, to a certain extent, because his mission was not one of war, but to carry provisions to the colony, and he had armed his vessels only for any

ROQUEMONT BLAMED

ordinary attack. Others, like Champlain, thought that Roquemont had unnecessarily exposed himself, and blame him for the following reasons:—(1.) The equipment was made out for helping the fort and habitation of Quebec. In facing combat Roquemont not only exposed himself to a loss, but also the whole country, that is to say about one hundred persons who were in distress. (2.) At Gaspé he was made aware that the English admiral had proceeded up the St. Lawrence in command of a fleet much more powerful than his own. He ought, therefore, to have taken the advice of his mariners in order to ascertain whether there was not a safe harbour along the coast which would have made a safe retreat. (3.) After having put his vessels in such a harbour, Roquemont ought to have sent a well equipped shallop to observe every movement of the enemy, and await his departure before going higher up the river. (4.) If Roquemont desired to fight, he ought to have laden the *Flibot* with flour and gunpowder, and placed on board the women and children, and this small ship, which was a fast sailer, could have escaped to Quebec during the fight. Champlain, in setting forth these views, is probably just, for the merit of a captain is not only in his courage, but also in his prudence. Nothing remained of the expedition under Roquemont, which was undertaken with so much courage, and at so much expense. It is certain that if he had been able to reach Quebec with his vessels, David Kirke

CHAMPLAIN

would not have risked, in the following year, the capture of the habitation of Quebec.

The king of England had granted letters patent to the Company of Adventurers which authorized them to trade, plant, seize Spanish and French vessels, and to destroy the forts of New France. By a singular coincidence the king of France had established the Company of New France at the same time, and they were thus constituted masters of commerce in Canada and Acadia.

Jarvis Kirke and others had equipped three vessels, to which were appointed David Kirke and his two brothers as captains. They stopped for a time at Miscou, and then entering the gulf and river St. Lawrence, they anchored at Tadousac, as we have already seen, during the first days of July, 1628. The news of Kirke's arrival soon reached Champlain, through an Indian named Napagabiscou, or Tregatin, who came in haste to Cape Tourmente. Foucher, the chief of the farmers, sent word at once to Quebec and appeared there himself not long afterwards to inform Champlain that the establishment had been burnt, his cattle destroyed, and all the inhabitants, save himself, taken prisoners. The prisoners were brought back to Quebec some days after accompanied by six Basques, who delivered to Champlain the following letter:

"MESSIEURS:—I give you notice that I have received a commission from the king of Great Britain, my honoured lord and master, to take possession of

A THREATENING MESSAGE

the countries of Canada and Acadia, and for that purpose eighteen ships have been despatched, each taking the route ordered by His Majesty. I have already seized the habitation of Miscou, and all boats and pinnaces on that coast, as well as those of Tadousac, where I am presently at anchor. You are also informed that among the vessels that I have seized, there is one belonging to the new company, commanded by a certain Noyrot, which was coming to you with provisions and goods for the trade. The Sieur de la Tour was also on board, whom I have taken into my ship. I was preparing to seek you, but thought it better to send boats to destroy and seize your cattle at Cape Tourmente; for I know that, when you are straightened for supplies, I shall the more easily obtain my desire, which is, to have your settlement; and in order that no vessels shall reach you, I have resolved to remain here till the end of the season, in order that you may not be re-victualled. Therefore see what you wish to do, if you intend to deliver up the settlement or not, for, God aiding, sooner or later I must have it. I would desire, for your sake, that it should be by courtesy rather than by force, to avoid the blood which might be spilt on both sides. By surrendering courteously, you may be assured of all kinds of contentment, both for your persons and for your property, which on the faith that I have in Paradise, I will preserve as I would my own, without the least portion in the world being diminished.

CHAMPLAIN

The Basques whom I send you are men of the vessels that I have captured, and they can tell you the state of affairs between France and England, and even how matters are passing in France, touching the new company of this country. Send me word what you desire to do, and if you wish to treat with me about this affair, send me a person to that effect, whom, I assure you, I will treat with all kinds of attention, and I will grant all reasonable demands that you may desire in resolving to give up the settlement. Waiting your reply, I remain, messieurs, your affectionate servant,

"DAVID QUER.

"On board the *Vicaille*, July 18th, 1628, and addressed to Monsieur Champlain, Commandant at Quebec."

Champlain read that letter to Pont-Gravé and to the chief inhabitants. After mature deliberation, it was resolved that Champlain should answer Kirke with dignity and firmness, but should not give any idea of the poor state of Quebec. "We concluded," says Champlain, "that if Kirke wished to see us he had better come, and not threaten from such a distance. That we did not in the least doubt the fact of Kirke having the commission of his king, as great princes always select men of brave and generous courage."

Champlain acknowledged the intelligence of the capture of Father Noyrot and de la Tour, and also the truth of the observation that the more pro-

NO SURRENDER

visions there were in a fortress the better it could hold out, still it could be maintained with but little, provided good order were kept; therefore, being still furnished with grain, maize. beans and pease, (besides what the country could supply) which his soldiers loved as well as the finest corn in the world, by surrendering the fort in so good a condition, he would be unworthy to appear before his sovereign, and would deserve chastisement before God and men. He was sure that Kirke would respect him much more for defending himself than for abandoning his charge, without first making trial of the English guns and batteries. Champlain concludes by saying that he would expect his attack, and oppose, as well as he could, all attempts that might be made against the place. The noble language of Champlain's letter made a deep impression on Kirke, and he deemed it prudent to start for Europe. Before leaving Tadousac, David Kirke destroyed all the captured French barques, with the exception of the largest, which he took to Europe. Since leaving England he had doubled the number of his vessels, having taken away all that he could from the habitation of Miscou and other seaports frequented by the French.

The news of the departure of the English fleet took some days to reach Quebec, where the minds of the inhabitants were divided between hope and fear. Champlain was determined to await the arrival of the enemy, and to defend Quebec, without considering its weakness. Every one began to work to construct new intrenchments around the habitation, and to barricade the road which led to the fort. Each was given a post in the event of an attack, and a defence was determined upon. Later on Champlain was informed of Roquemont's fate and of Kirke's departure.

The English were, indeed, well compensated for their abandonment of Quebec, for the seizure of the vessels and their provisions was equivalent to the capture of the French colony, since famine threatened them sooner or later. In attacking Quebec Kirke, indeed, would have met with but little opposition, because every one was suffering. Those who could have lived from the produce of their own lands, were compelled to give assistance to the trade agents. Champlain ordered a distribution of pease to be made to each person indiscriminately. The Récollets refused any assistance, and they passed the whole winter subsisting on corn and vegetables of their own cultivation. Champlain succeeded in building a mill for grinding pease. The eel fisheries were productive, and the Indians sold to the French six eels for a beaver skin. In the midst of these perplexities Champlain realized that unless assistance was forthcoming in the spring, it would be advisable for him to accept an honourable capitulation, and to send all the French who wished to return to their country, either to Gaspé or to Miscou.

PONT-GRAVÉ'S COMMISSION

As soon as the snow had disappeared in the spring of the year 1629, Champlain caused all the arable land to be sown. By the middle of May his stock of provisions was nearly exhausted, and he therefore decided to send Desdames to Gaspé to seek aid for Quebec there from the inhabitants or any French ships he might meet. One month later Desdames returned, and confirmed the news that the English vessels had devastated the Acadian coast, and burnt the habitations. Neither Desdames nor his party had seen any French vessel in the gulf, but they had met Iuan Chou, a friend of Champlain, who had agreed to give hospitality to twenty persons, including Pont-Gravé, by whom he was greatly esteemed. The latter was still suffering from gout, and it was with some reluctance that he agreed to leave his position as first clerk, empowered by Guillaume de Caën to take care of the merchandise. Des Mertes, who was Pont-Gravé's grandson, accepted his position in the interim.

Before leaving Quebec Pont-Gravé desired Champlain to read publicly the commission which he had received from Guillaume de Caën. After grand mass on June 17th Champlain read Pont-Gravé's commission and his own in the presence of all the people, and he added some words, by which it was easily understood that the king's authority had to be superior to Guillaume de Caën's commissions. Pont-Gravé replied at once: "I see that you believe in the nullity of my commission!" "Yes," replied Champlain, "when it comes in conflict with the king's and the viceroy's authority." This petty dispute had no serious consequence, as it was evident that Pont-Gravé, being only the first clerk of Guillaume de Caën, had no other authority than to take care of the peltry and merchandise belonging to his chief.

Before turning their attention to Canada Guillaume and Emery de Caën had belonged to a large company trading with the East Indies. Both were Calvinists. Sagard writes that Guillaume was polite, liberal, and of good understanding. This testimony seems somewhat exaggerated, as we have many proofs of his niggardliness. His nephew Emery was frank, liberal and open to conviction, and was always kindly disposed towards the Jesuits. Guillaume de Caën was the commodore of the fleet equipped by his associates. His greatest fault appears to have been that he neglected Champlain and the colony, and for that reason he should share the responsibility of not having prevented the capitulation of Quebec. However, it is scarcely fair to say of him that he worked directly against the French in New France. After the capitulation of 1629, Cardinal Richelieu wrote of him to the French ambassador in London: "Please examine his actions. Being a Huguenot, and having been much displeased with the new company of Canada, I have entertained a suspicion that he connived with the English. I have

EMERY DE CAËN

not a sure knowledge of it, but you will please me if you inform me of his conduct."

This suspicion seems unfounded, because Guillaume de Caën was personally interested in the fate of Quebec. His merchandise which was seized by Kirke was valued at about forty thousand écus. If he had made some agreement with Kirke he would have had no difficulty in recovering his goods after the capitulation, but such was not the case.

As to Emery de Caën we must say that he took an active part in the defence of the colony, and perhaps he might have saved Quebec, had not one of his sailors committed a grave imprudence at a critical juncture. The facts are as follows: The Treaty of Susa, which was signed on April 24th, 1629, had established peace between France and England. Being aware of this fact Emery de Caën equipped a vessel for the purpose of bringing back to France all the furs and merchandise which were the property of his uncle. When he arrived near the Escoumins a dense fog obscured the coast, and his vessel ran aground on Red Island, opposite Tadousac. Having succeeded in floating his ship, de Caën went to Chafaud aux Basques, two leagues above Tadousac. Here he was informed that the Kirke brothers were at Tadousac, and he at once made for Mal Bay, where he was informed that Champlain had capitulated. This news lacked confirmation, and so he sent two emissaries to Quebec, who instead of proceeding directly there, amused

CHAMPLAIN

themselves on the shore of the river at Cape Tourmente. They finally arrived at their destination, and were badly received by Guillaume Couillard.

In the meantime Thomas Kirke was sailing down from Quebec to Tadousac, after the capitulation of the stronghold, and meeting de Caën's vessel approached within cannon shot. A fight began, and soon both vessels were stopped by Kirke's order. Previous to this, Champlain and all the French who were on board had been sent below deck, the covers of which had been fastened with large nails, so that they were unable to render any assistance to Emery de Caën, even if they had desired to. The battle continued under some difficulties, and the vessels were grappled only near the bowsprit of Caën's vessel. The combat continued indecisively for some time until Kirke finally secured the victory, in part because of a singular blunder. One of Emery de Caën's sailors having cried "*Quartier! Quartier!*" or Surrender! Kirke hurriedly answered, "*Bon quartier*, and I promise your life safe, and I shall treat you as I did Champlain, whom I bring with me." Hearing these words the French hesitated, ceased firing, and soon perceived Champlain on the deck. Kirke had released him from his temporary jail, threatening him with death if the men of Emery de Caën fired again. Then Champlain said: "It would be easy to kill me, being in your power. But you would not deserve honour for having broken your

DE CAËN SURRENDERS

word. You have promised to treat me with consideration. I cannot command these people nor prevent them from doing their duty, in defending themselves. You should praise them instead of blaming them." Champlain advised them to surrender on terms. They were wise in doing so, as two English *pataches* soon arrived which would have settled the fight.

Emery de Caën, and Jacques Couillard de l'Espinay, his lieutenant, were taken on to Kirke's vessel, and submitted themselves to the enemy's conditions. De Caën was compelled to abandon his ship, which was full of provisions intended for Quebec. In less than two hours every hope of fur trading had disappeared. De Caën had lost not only his vessel, but also five hundred beaver skins and some merchandise for traffic. The loss was valued at fifty-one thousand francs. Emery de Caën returned to France. He came back to Quebec in the year 1631, with permission from Richelieu to treat with the Indians. But the English commander expressly forbade the trade, and placed guardians on his vessel during the period of trading.

CHAPTER X

THE CAPITULATION OF QUEBEC, 1629

WE have somewhat anticipated events, so we now retrace our steps, and place ourselves within Champlain's defenceless stronghold as its fatal hour approached. On Thursday, July 19th, 1629, a savage named La Nasse by the French, and Manitougatche by his own people, informed the Jesuits that three English ships were in sight off the Island of Orleans, behind Point Lévis, and that six other vessels were anchored at Tadousac. Champlain was already aware that some ships were at Tadousac, but he was surprised to learn that the enemy had approached Quebec, and at first he thought that they might be French ships. There was no one in Fort St. Louis at the time he received this news, as every one had gone out in search of plants which were used as food; he therefore consulted with the Récollet and Jesuit fathers, and others of note as to what measures should be taken. In the meantime the English ships were steadily approaching, and at length drew up at a certain distance from the city. A shallop was then sent out from the admiral's ship, carrying at her mainmast a white flag. Champlain caused a similar flag to be run up over the fort, and Kirke's emissary came ashore and presented to Champlain the following letter:—

"MONSIEUR:—In consequence of what our brother told you last year that sooner or later he would have Quebec, if not succoured, he has charged us to assure you of his friendship as we do of ours; and knowing very well the extreme need of everything in which you are, desires that you shall surrender the fort and the settlement to us, assuring you of every kind of courtesy for you and yours, and also of honourable and reasonable terms, such as you may wish. Waiting your reply, we remain, monsieur, your very affectionate servants,

"LOUIS AND THOMAS QUER.

"On board the *Flibot*, this July 19th, 1629."

Champlain immediately prepared his answer, the terms of which had previously been agreed upon in consultation. Kirke's representative did not understand a word of the French language, but he had a fair knowledge of Latin. Father de la Roche d'Aillon was therefore requested by Champlain to act as interpreter, and he asked the following questions:—"Is war declared between France and England?" "No," replied the English representative. "Why, then, do you come here to trouble us if our princes live in peace?" he was asked.

Champlain then requested Father de la Roche to go aboard the English vessels to ascertain from the chiefs what they intended to do. The interview between Father de la Roche and Louis Kirke was

DE LA ROCHE'S INTERVIEW

courteous, but the answers of the latter were far from being satisfactory. "If Champlain," said the English captain, "gives up the keys of the fortress and of the habitation we promise to convey you all to France, and will treat you well; if not we will oblige him by force." Father de la Roche tried to obtain fifteen days' delay, or even eight days, but it was of no avail.

"Sir," said Louis Kirke, "I well know your miserable condition. Your people have gone out to pick up roots in order to avoid starvation, for we have captured Master Boullé and some other Frenchmen whom we have retained as prisoners at Tadousac, and from whom we have ascertained the condition of the inhabitants of Quebec."

"Give us a delay of eight days," said Father de la Roche. "No," replied Thomas Kirke, "I shall at once ruin the fort with my cannon." "I desire to sleep to-night in the fort," added his brother Louis, "and, if not, I shall devastate the whole country." "Proceed slowly," said Father de la Roche, "for you are deceived if you believe you will easily gain the fort. There are a hundred men there well armed and ready to sell their lives dearly. Perchance you will find your death in this enterprise, for I assure you that the inhabitants are determined to fight, and they derive courage from the conviction that your invasion is unjust, and that their lives and property are at stake. Once more I warn you that an attack might prove dangerous to you."

CHAMPLAIN

Captain Louis Kirke seemed a little disheartened on hearing this firm and vigorous language. After having consulted the chief officers of his fleet he asked Father de la Roche to attend a council of war at which an ultimatum was presented in these words:—" Champlain must surrender at once, but he shall have the privilege of dictating the terms of capitulation." Three hours were granted within which his reply was to be given. The Récollets were promised protection, but no conditions were accorded to the Jesuits, as it was the admiral's intention to visit their convent, which he believed to contain a quantity of beaver skins.

Father de la Roche returned to Fort St. Louis, and gave an account of his interview. It was plainly evident that it would be useless to rely upon delays in the face of an enemy determined to see the end of the affair. Food was almost exhausted, and it was calculated that there were not more than ten pounds of flour in Quebec, and not more than fifty pounds of gunpowder, which was of inferior quality. Opposition would have been not only useless, but ridiculous. Champlain realized this, and at once resolved to surrender.

Champlain drew up the following articles of capitulation, which were forwarded to the Kirke brothers:—

"That Quer (Kirke) should produce his commission from the king of England to prove that war actually existed between England and France; and

ARTICLES OF CAPITULATION

also to show his power from his brother, who commanded the fleet, to treat with Champlain.

"That a vessel should be provided to convey Champlain, his companions, the missionaries, both Jesuits and Récollets, the two Indian girls that had been given to him two years before, and all other persons, to France.

"That the religious and other people should be allowed to leave with arms and baggage, and all their furniture, and that a sufficient supply of provisions for the passage to France should be granted in exchange for peltry, etc.

"That all should have the most favourable treatment possible, without violence to any.

"That the ship in which they were to embark for France should be ready in three days after their arrival at Tadousac, and a vessel provided for the transport of their goods, etc., to that place."

These articles were signed by Champlain and Pont-Gravé. After having read them Louis Kirke sent this answer: "That Kirke's commission should be shown and his powers to his brothers for trading purposes. As to providing a vessel to take Champlain and his people direct to France, that could not be done, but they would give them passage to England, and from there to France, whereby they would avoid being again taken by any English cruiser on their route. For the Indian girls, that clause could not be granted, for reasons which would be explained. As to leaving with arms and baggage, the officers might take with them their arms, clothes, and peltries belonging to them, and the soldiers might have their clothes and a beaver robe each. As for the holy fathers, they must be contented with their robes and books.

"L. KIRKE.

"THOMAS KIRKE.

"The said articles granted to Champlain and Du Pont, I accept and ratify them, and I promise that they shall be executed from point to point. Done at Tadousac, August 19th (new style), 1629.

"DAVID KIRKE."

The clause forbidding the soldiers to take their arms, coats and peltry, excepting a castor robe, was a severe trial to them, as many of them had bought skins from the Hurons to the extent of seven to eight hundred francs, and preferred to fight rather than lose their fortune.

Champlain had agreed to capitulate without firing. Some openly reproached Champlain, saying that it was not the fear of death that actuated his course, but rather the loss of the thousand livres, which the English had agreed to give him if he abandoned Quebec without striking a blow.

Champlain was informed of all the murmurs and discontent which were expressed amongst his people by a young Greek, who was charged to inform him that they did not wish to surrender, and even if they lost their fort, they desired to prove to the English that they were full of courage. Champlain

BROTHER SAGARD'S OPINION

was annoyed at these exhibitions of insubordination, and he instructed the Greek to give the people this answer:—"You are badly advised and unwise. How can you desire resistance when we have no provisions, no ammunition, or any prospect of relief? Are you tired of living, or do you expect to be victorious under such circumstances? Obey those who desire your safety and who do nothing without prudence."

Brother Sagard makes these remarks upon the condition of affairs:—"It is true that there was a great scarcity of all things necessary for the habitation, but the enemy, too, were weak, as Father Joseph perceived after having examined the whole crew, which consisted of about two hundred soldiers, for the most part, men who had never touched a musket, and who could have been killed as ducks or who would have run away. Moreover they were in a wretched condition, and of a low order. The weather was favourable to the French, as the tide was low, and there was a strong southwest wind, which drove the enemy ships in the direction of France, so that there was no assurance for either the vessels or the barques. Champlain, however, deemed it more expedient to surrender than to run the risk of losing lives or of being made prisoner while defending a fort so badly armed."

If, as the veracious Brother Sagard says, the fort and the habitation were in such straits, it is not proved that the English could be easily defeated.

CHAMPLAIN

There were at Quebec only fifty men capable of bearing arms, and only a small quantity of gunpowder in store, while provisions were absolutely wanting. How was it possible to sustain a siege without ammunition, without bread and without soldiers?

On the enemy's side there were three vessels, one well equipped, and nearly two hundred men. If the men were desperate or wretched, they would be the more dangerous. Even supposing that the two vessels had proved insufficient for a protracted siege, the four vessels at the disposal of David Kirke would have surely come to their assistance.

It would have been a foolish act to have resisted such a powerful enemy. Besides, Champlain had another foe to contend against, for Nicholas Marsolet, Étienne Brûlé, Pierre Reye, and others, had betrayed him, and were leagued with Kirke. Champlain understood the difficulties of his position, and his responsibilities, for he had in his hands the lives of all those at Quebec.

Of the eighty persons living in Quebec at this time, two-thirds had only private interests to safeguard, and it was a matter of indifference to them whether they remained in Canada or whether they returned to France. The families who had nothing to gain by leaving Quebec were those who deserved the governor's sympathy, and it was for their safety that Champlain would not agree to offer resistance as the result must have proved disas-

SURRENDERING THE KEYS

trous to them. By the articles of capitulation these families would be able to live quietly at home, awaiting the issue of affairs from Europe.

On the day following the preliminaries, Champlain went on board Louis Kirke's vessel, where he was to see the commission from David Kirke, empowering the Kirke brothers to take Quebec and the whole country by assault. Both parties then signed the articles of capitulation, and the English troops, conducted by Champlain, came in shallops near to the habitation. The keys were delivered to Louis Kirke, and then they all proceeded to the fort, which was delivered to the captain. Quebec was definitely put under the authority of the English, who had not fired a single shot. Louis Kirke placed Le Baillif, who had been dismissed by Guillaume de Caën for his bad conduct, in charge of the storehouse. This was the first reward for his treason. Champlain asked the English commander to protect the chapel of Quebec, the convents, and the houses of the widow of Louis Hébert and of her son-in-law, Guillaume Couillard, and he offered him the keys of his own room within the fort. Louis Kirke refused to accept the latter, and left Champlain in possession of his room. This courteous action was followed by another one, for Kirke delivered to Champlain a certificate of all that he had found within the fort and the habitation. This document was found useful later on, when it was necessary to settle the value of the goods.

CHAMPLAIN

In the meantime the English crew robbed the convent of the Jesuits, but they did not find the beaver skins, as they expected. Kirke and the Lutheran minister took for their own use some of the choicest volumes of the library, and three or four pictures. The Récollets had filled a leather bag with the ornaments of their church, and had hidden it under ground, far in the woods, thinking that they might return sooner or later.

On the Sunday following the capitulation, July 22nd, Louis Kirke hoisted the English flag over one of the bastions of the fort, and in order to render the official possession of Quebec more imposing, he placed his soldiers in ranks along the ramparts, and at a precise hour a volley was fired from English muskets. Two day later, Champlain, with some companions, took passage on the *Flibot* for Tadousac, leaving behind the families of Couillard, Martin, Desportes, Hébert, Hubou, Pivert, Duchesne the surgeon, some interpreters and clerks, and Pont-Gravé, who was too sick to leave his room. It was understood that all those who desired to return to France should start on the day fixed by Kirke.

The fate of the colony was thus decided. Those who had any authority, by reason of their work or their official position, were compelled to leave. The others were at liberty to remain, especially the interpreters, who would be useful in trading with the Indians. Before Champlain's departure,

A FEW REMAIN

some had asked his advice. Should they remain in Quebec under a new régime, with little to hope for? Who was this victorious Kirke, so captivating in appearance? Perhaps a lion clothed with the skin of a lamb! They knew the Kirke brothers had been guilty of burning the habitation at Cape Tourmente. Knowing that they were Protestants, they could not expect sympathy on the score of religion. A danger existed from every point of view. Nevertheless, Champlain advised many of them to remain at Quebec in order to save their property. The only objection was that they would be obliged to remain for an indefinite time without the ministrations of their priests.

Three years were to elapse before a French vessel again appeared at Quebec, with authority to hoist the white flag of France. Champlain's advice was not prejudicial to any one, at least not in temporal matters. This small nucleus became the great tree whose branches and leaves extend to-day over the whole American continent. If France had seen the complete depopulation of Canada, perhaps the king would not have made the same efforts to have his colony restored. Champlain himself, in spite of his great zeal and his love for the country which he had founded had been discouraged by the difficulties. He could foresee better than any other the obstacles which the future would present and it caused him much uneasiness, and offered little consolation. At his age most men would have preferred to rest after an agitated life of thirty years, in the pursuit of an idea which it seemed impossible to realize on account of the manifold difficulties by which it was constantly beset.

CHAPTER XI

THE LAST EVENTS OF 1629

"SINCE the English have taken possession of Quebec," writes Champlain, "the days have seemed to me as long as months." This dreariness is easily explained. The unsettled state of affairs, of which he was an eye-witness, had rendered his life at Quebec intolerable. Louis Kirke, however, treated him with respect and courtesy, and had given him permission to bring to Tadousac his two adopted girls, Espérance and Charité. It was a favour wholly unexpected, especially as by one of the clauses of the act of capitulation he was denied passage for them. Champlain, however, was ready to buy their liberty, if necessary, as he wished to civilize them and convert them to Christianity. Having no desire to stay longer in a place where even the beauties of the sunset seemed to remind him of his humiliation, Champlain only resided temporarily at Tadousac, and was anxious to reach France. He had left Quebec on July 24th, and on the following day he perceived a vessel sailing near Murray Bay. This was Emery de Caën's ship, which, as we have already stated, was proceeding to Quebec to claim the peltry in the storehouse which belonged to his uncle. This vessel, as has been described, was captured by Kirke.

CHAMPLAIN

A certain Captain Daniel likewise failed to relieve Quebec. He had crossed the ocean from Dieppe with four vessels and a barque laden with provisions and ammunition. Having heard on the passage that a Scottish lord named James Stuart, had erected a fort on Cape Breton, in a place called Port-aux-Baleines, to protect his countrymen during the fishing season, Daniel went out of his way to destroy this fort, and to build one at Grand Cibou to check the intruders, instead of preceeding directly to Quebec, as was his duty. He left at this place forty men and two Jesuits, Father Vimont and Father de Vieux-Pont, and then, having set up the arms of France, he returned to his country without having done anything for the Quebec habitation. This was his first fault, but nevertheless it was a great misfortune for Quebec.

The Jesuits had prepared at a great expense a shipment for Quebec. Father Noyrot brought with him Father Charles Lalement, who was returning after an absence of nearly two years, Father de Vieux-Pont, Brother Louis Malot and twenty-four persons. Driven by a terrible storm, their barque was wrecked near the Island of Canseau. Fourteen were drowned, including Father Noyrot and Brother Malot. The others miraculously escaped.

The Chevalier de Razilly was finally ordered to assist Quebec, but when it was found that peace had been concluded between France and England

A RELIGIOUS DISPUTE

on April 24th, Razilly had his commission cancelled and proceeded to Morocco.

The failure of these three expeditions, together with that of Emery de Caën, occurring at the same time under unfortunate circumstances, resulted in the loss of the colony for France, and won at least temporary prestige and importance for the Kirke family.

Champlain relates some remarkable events during his sojourn at Tadousac. Religious fanaticism displayed itself in its worst form. The French had with them Father de Brébeuf, who was quite competent and willing to champion the cause of the Catholic faith and especially when assailed by his own countrymen. A French Huguenot, named Jacques Michel, apparently headed a crusade against the Jesuits. One day Kirke said to a party that the Jesuits had come to Canada to annoy the Sieurs de Caën in their trade. "I beg your pardon," replied the father, "we had no other design in coming here than the glory of God and the conversion of the savages." To which Jacques Michel retorted, still more audaciously: "Yes, convert the savages, say rather, convert the beavers." "It is false," replied the priest, somewhat vexed. Michel, who was angry, raised his arm to strike the father, at the same time saying: "If I were not restrained by the respect due to my chief, I would slap your face for your denial." "I ask your pardon,' said the father, "it was not in my mind to injure you, and if my answer has vexed you, I regret it." Michel was not satisfied and began to blaspheme, so that Champlain was scandalized, and said: "You swear much for a Reformer." "It is true," replied the Huguenot, "but I am furious against this Jesuit for his denial, and if I hang to-morrow I will give him the blows he deserves." During the day, however, Michel drank heavily and was attacked by apoplexy, from which he died thirty-five hours later, without exhibiting any signs of repentance.

The commander Kirke "wished," says Champlain, "to show a last proof of his friendship. So instead of having Michel quietly buried, he ordered a splendid funeral, accompanied with military honours. When the remains were lowered into the grave, a salute of eighty guns was fired, as if the deceased had been an officer of high rank. Whatever may have been the reasons for showing these tokens of honour to the remains of Michel, the savages seem to have resented the proceedings, for they later unearthed his body and gave it to the dogs. Michel had been a traitor to his country and to his God, and this was the method of his punishment.

We have already mentioned the names of the Frenchmen who betrayed Champlain, particularly Étienne Brûlé, Le Baillif, Pierre Reye and Marsolet. Let us examine their conduct. Étienne Brûlé, in his capacity of interpreter, had rendered many good services to his compatriots. Unfortunately, his private actions while dwelling with the Hurons

BRÛLÉ AND MARSOLET

were not above reproach, and he would certainly have been compelled to expiate his offences had he not been adopted as one of their family. Brûlé worked for the benefit of the Hurons, and their gratitude towards a good officer perhaps outweighed their memory of an injury. On retiring from the Huron country in 1629, Brûlé went to Tadousac, where he entered the service of Kirke, and some years after he was killed by a savage.

Marsolet's case is nearly identical with that of Brûlé, although it is not proved that he was as licentious during the time that he lived with the Algonquins. He and Brûlé asserted that they were compelled by Kirke to serve under the British flag. Champlain severely blamed their conduct, saying: "Remember that God will punish you if you do not amend your lives. You have lost your honour. Wherever you will go, men will point at you, saying: 'These are the men who have threatened their king and sold their country.' It would be preferable to die than to live on in this manner, as you will suffer the remorse of a bad conscience." To this they replied: "We well know that in France we should be hanged. We are sorry for what has happened, but it is done and we must drain the cup to the bottom, and resolve never to return to France." Champlain answered them: "If you are captured anywhere, you will run the risk of being chastised as you deserve."

Nicholas Marsolet became a good citizen, and his

family alliances were the most honourable. Pierre Reye, a carriage maker, was a bad character, "One of the worst traitors, and wicked." His treason did not surprise any one, and nothing better was expected of him. Le Baillif was not only vicious, but a thief. On the night after the seizure by Kirke of the goods in store, he took from the room of Corneille de Vendremur, a clerk, one hundred livres in gold and money, a silver cup and some silk stockings. He was suspected of having stolen from the chapel of the Lower Town, a silver chalice, the gift of Anne of Austria. Though he was a Catholic, Le Baillif ate food on days of abstinence, in order to please the Protestants. He treated the French as if they were dogs. "I shall abandon him," says Champlain, "to his fate, awaiting the day of his punishment for his swearings, cursings and impieties."

The treachery of these four men greatly affected Champlain, who was at a loss to understand how those to whom he had given food and shelter could be so ungrateful; but their conduct, however reprehensible, played no part in the loss of the colony. Kirke employed them to further his purposes without giving them any substantial reward.

The sojourn of the French in Tadousac lasted many weeks, and the delay caused Champlain much annoyance. David Kirke spent ten or twelve days on his visit to Quebec, where he wanted to see for himself how his brother Louis had disposed of

A BANQUET AT TADOUSAC

everything, and what advantage he was likely to gain from the acquisition of the new country. Believing himself to be the supreme ruler and master of New France, he outlined a brilliant future for the colony, looking forward to the day when he could bring settlers to take advantage of its natural resources.

Returning to Tadousac, the general invited his captains to a dinner, at which Champlain was also a guest. The dinner was served in a tent surrounded with branches. Towards the end of the banquet David Kirke gave Champlain a letter from Marsolet to inform him that the chief savages, gathered at Three Rivers in council, had resolved to keep with them the two girls, Espérance and Charité. This was a severe trial to Champlain, who had hoped to be able to take them to France. All his efforts, however, were useless, as there was a plot organized by the traitor Marsolet. These children loved Champlain as a father, and were inconsolable when they realized that their departure for France was impossible.

Champlain relates many things that do not redound to Kirke's credit, amongst other things that Kirke blamed his brother Louis for giving the Jesuits permission to say mass, and afterwards refused the permission. Again, at the moment when the Jesuits embarked for Tadousac, Louis Kirke ordered a trunk to be opened in which the sacred vessels were contained. Seeing a box which contained a chalice Kirke tried to seize it, but Father Massé interfered, and said to him: "This is a sacred object, do not profane it, if you please." "Why," said Kirke, "we have no faith in your superstition," and so saying he took the chalice in his hands, braving the Jesuit's advice. The Catholics were also denied the privilege of praying in public. This intolerant action was condemned by Champlain. During their stay at Tadousac Champlain and the admiral went out shooting. They killed more than two thousand larks, plovers, snipes and curlews. In the meantime the sailors had cut trees for masts, and some birch which they took to England. They also carried with them four thousand five hundred and forty beaver skins, one thousand seven hundred and thirteen others seized at Quebec, and four hundred and thirty-two elk skins. The French had not given up all their skins; some had hidden a good many, and others kept them with Kirke's consent. The Récollets and the Jesuits were returning poorer than when they came. Champlain alone was allowed to retain all his baggage. At the commencement of September the admiral fitted out a medium sized barque with provisions for Quebec, with instructions to bring back the Récollets who were scattered throughout the country, and also some of the French who had intended to remain at Quebec and other places.

On September 14th the English fleet set out carrying Champlain, the Jesuits, the Récollets, and two-thirds of the French, that is to say, nearly the

THE FATHERS REACH FRANCE

whole of the colony. The passage was short though difficult, and eleven of the crew died from dysentery. On October 20th the vessels reached Plymouth where Kirke was much disappointed to learn that the treaty of peace signed on April 24th had been confirmed on September 16th. All the French, except Champlain, took passage for France at Dover. Champlain proceeded directly to London, where he met the French ambassador, M. de Chateauneuf, and related to him the events which had taken place in Canada, and urged him to take steps for its restoration to France.

The fathers disembarked at Calais at the end of October. Father Massé returned to his former position of minister at the college of La Flèche. Father Anne de Noüe went to Bourges. Father de Brébeuf entered the college of Rouen, where he had laboured previously, and three other Jesuits whom we find afterwards in Canada, Father Charles Lalemant, Father Jogues and Father Simon Lemoyne, were at that time professors in this college. Father Massé and Father de Brébeuf were soon to resume their ministration in this country, which they were forced to abandon at a time when they had hoped to see the realization of their noble mission. L'Abbé Faillon has written that the family of Hébert alone remained at Quebec after the surrender, but this seems uncertain. It may be that other families remained in Quebec. It was God's will that the most prominent and influential men

CHAMPLAIN

should leave for France, but He also ordained that a few heroic settlers or possessors of New France should remain. If their remaining was favourable to France Champlain deserves the credit, for he did more that any of his countrymen to bring it about. The population of Quebec or of the whole colony in July, 1629, was divided as follows:—Inhabitants, twenty-three; interpreters, eleven; clerks, fourteen; missionaries, ten; domestics, seven; French, arrived from the Huron country, twenty. This makes a total number of eighty-five persons.

The following probably remained at Quebec:— Guillaume Hubou and his wife, Marie Rollet, widow of Louis Hébert; Guillaume Hébert; Guillaume Couillard, and his wife Guillemette Hébert, and their three children; Abraham Martin, and his wife, Marguerite Langlois, and their three children; Pierre Desportes, and his wife, Françoise Langlois, and their daughter Hélène; Nicholas Pivert, his wife, Marguerite Lesage, and their niece; Adrien Duchesne and his wife; Jean Foucher, Étienne Brûlé, Nicholas Marsolet, Le Baillif, Pierre Reye, Olivier Le Tardif. The missionaries who returned to France were: Three Jesuits, two Récollets, two Brothers Jesuits and three Brothers Récollets, ten in all. Their names were Fathers Jesuits Enemond Massé, Anne de Noüe and Jean de Brébeuf; Fathers Récollets Joseph de la Roche d'Aillon, and Joseph Le Caron; Brothers Jesuits François Charton and Gilbert Burel; and the Récollet Friars Gervais

BIRTHS, MARRIAGES AND DEATHS

Mohier, Jean Gaufestre and Pierre Langoissieux. Among the clerks who returned home were Corneille de Vendremur, Thierry-Desdames, Eustache Boullé, and Destouches

Since the year 1608 there had been only seven births, three marriages, and forty deaths. One man had been hanged, six had been murdered, and three drowned. A Récollet father, called Nicholas Viel, had perished in the Sault au Récollet; and there had been sixteen victims of the scurvy.

CHAPTER XII

QUEBEC RESTORED

THROUGH the exertions of Champlain negotiations were soon entered into for the purpose of restoring the colony of New France to the French. Champlain had visited the French ambassador, M. de Chateauneuf, when in London, and had laid before him a statement of the events which had recently taken place, together with the treaty of capitulation and a map of New France, so far as it was explored. According to Champlain, the country comprised all the lands which Linschot thus describes: "This part of America which extends to the Arctic pole northward, is called New France, because Jean Verrazano, a Florentine, having been sent by King François I to these quarters, discovered nearly all the coast, beginning from the Tropic of Cancer to the fiftieth degree, and still more northerly, arboring arms and flags of France; for that reason the said country is called New France."

Champlain was not quarrelling with the English for Virginia, although this country had been sailed along by the French eighty years before, and they had also discovered the American coast, from the river St. John to the peninsula of Florida.

CHAMPLAIN

No one can deny that Champlain had given names to the rivers and harbours of New England as far as Cape Cod, about the fortieth degree of latitude.

After having spent about five weeks with the ambassador in furnishing him with information to guide him in his negotiations with the English authorities, Champlain resolved to visit France, as he had a reasonable hope of seeing his designs accomplished. He left London on November 30th, and embarked at Rye, in Sussex, for Dieppe. Here he met Captain Daniel, who had just returned from his expedition to Canada, and it was here also that he received his commission as governor of New France, which had been forwarded by the directors of the Company of New France.

Champlain paid a visit to Rouen, and then went to Paris, where he had interviews with the king, with the cardinal, and some of the associates of the company. A prominent topic of discussion was, naturally, the loss of New France, and the best means of recovering it. Champlain bent all his energies to secure this end and to gain the support of all those interested in the fate of New France.

Events progressed favourably, and Champlain was pleased to learn that Doctor Daniel had been sent to London with letters for King Charles I. Louis XIII demanded the restoration of the fort and habitation of Quebec, and the forts and harbours of the Acadian coast, for the reason that they had been captured after peace had been con-

THE RESTORATION OF CANADA

cluded between the two countries. Doctor Daniel returned to France, bearing despatches by which Charles I answered that he was ready to restore Quebec, but no mention was made of Acadia. The directors of the company immediately ordered Commander de Razilly to equip a fleet, and to take possession of Quebec by force or otherwise.

The Hundred Associates subscribed sixteen thousand livres for the freighting of the vessels, and the king granted the balance of the expenses. The news of these extraordinary war-like preparations caused alarm in London, but the French ambassador stated that these vessels were being sent as escort to the traders, not to trouble the English settlers who had taken possession of the French habitations. This explanation relieved the public mind in England, and Charles I promised to give back to France its ancient possessions in America, as they were on April 24th, 1629, the date of the signing of the Treaty of Susa. In justice to England it may be said that two English vessels were seized by the French at about the same time that Kirke had forced Champlain to surrender. There was, therefore, illegal action on both sides, and both countries had claims to be regulated.

The English would have preferred to have retained possession of Canada, at least until the following year, as the Kirke brothers and their associates hoped to be able to realize considerable sums from their trade with the Indians. This condition of affairs is explained in a letter addressed by Cardinal Richelieu to Chateauneuf, on December 20th, 1629: "They assure us that they cannot restore Canada at once; this is the reason for our delay in restoring these vessels." And he adds: "If they agree to the restitution of Quebec without any condition, you shall accept it; if not, it is better to put a delay to the settlement."

It is obvious that Charles I had twice promised to restore Quebec, and when Chateauneuf retired from his position of ambassador in the month of April, 1630, he had obtained "every assurance of restitution of all things taken since the peace." The Marquis of Fontenay-Mareuil, who succeeded Chateauneuf on March 13th, received special instructions from the cardinal on this subject: "His Majesty's design is that, continuing the negotiations of Chateauneuf, you continue to ask for the restitution of Canada, and of all goods and vessels taken from the French since the peace."

The new ambassador could not urge the claims of France with greater activity than his predecessor. During the space of two months, Chateauneuf had prepared five documents relating to Canadian affairs to which the commissioners appointed to settle the matter had replied on February 11th. These officials were Sir Humphrey May, Sir John Coke, Sir Julius Cæsar, and Sir Henry Martin. Their conclusion regarding Canada was that His

TERMS OF RESTITUTION

Majesty had not changed his mind concerning the restoration of places, vessels and goods taken from the French, according to the first declaration he had made through a memorandum in Latin, communicated some time since to the French ambassador.

Louis XIII was at this time engaged in war with Austria, and Richelieu was too busy to attend to Canadian matters, which were of less importance than the European questions which occupied his time. Interior dissensions were soon added to the trouble which France had to undergo. Gaston, the king's brother, was compromised, and the Duke of Montmorency, who took part in a plot against the king, was seized and put to death.

The negotiations commenced in 1629 were not resumed until 1632. In the meantime the English authorities had not been idle. Charles I had not forgotten his promise, and even if he had, there were men in France who had a good memory. On June 12th, 1631, Charles I addressed a long letter to Sir Isaac Wake, ambassador to France, respecting the restitution of Quebec and Acadia. A paragraph summarises the English claims as follows:

"That which we require, is the payment of the remainder of the marriage dowry, the restitution of certain ships taken and kept without any colour or pretence, and the withdrawal of arrests and seizures which were made in that kingdom against our subjects contrary to treaty, being of right and due. And that which is demanded of us concerning the places in Canada and those parts, and some few ships of that nation (French) which remain yet unrestored, but have had sentence of confiscation passed upon them in our high Court of Admiralty upon good grounds in justice, these are things of courtesy and good will.

According to her marriage settlement the Queen Henrietta possessed a dowry of eight hundred thousand crowns, equivalent to eight hundred thousand crowns of three livres, French currency. The half of that sum had been made payable on the day before the marriage in London and the other half a year later. The marriage took place on June 13th, 1625, and the first instalment was then paid. In the year 1631 the second instalment had not been paid, and Charles I claimed it as one of the conditions of settlement.

Some historians have stated that the king took this opportunity to have a money question solved. If, however, the debt was legitimate, France was obliged to pay it, and the difficulties that had occurred in the meantime had nothing to do with the deed of marriage upon which the claim was based. Chateauneuf had promised to pay the claim. Unless, therefore, there was any doubt as to the right of the king to claim the sum, it is difficult to understand why the king should be blamed.

In his letter to his ambassador at Paris Charles I alludes to documents exchanged between Chateauneuf and Fontenay-Mareuil on the one side, and the

VALUE OF THE PELTRY

lords commissioners appointed to give a ruling. In this document it is noticed that Guillaume de Caën had discussed with Kirke the value of the goods and peltry that had been taken out of the stores at Quebec. They disagreed both as to the number and value. De Caën claimed four thousand two hundred and sixty-six beaver skins which had been captured by Kirke, while Kirke declared he had found only one thousand seven hundred and thirteen, and that the balance of his cargo, four thousand skins, was the result of trade with the Indians.

According to the books of the English company, Kirke had bought four thousand five hundred and forty beaver skins, four hundred and thirty-two elk skins, and had found in the stores one thousand seven hundred and thirteen beaver skins. The difference in the calculation is due to the fact that the English only mentioned the beaver skins registered in their books, and the French included all the skins which belonged to them when the fort surrendered, making no mention of those that they hid or took out of the fort with the permission of the English. Guillaume de Caën valued each skin at thirty-seven shillings and sixpence, and Burlamachi had written from Metz to representatives of the English company, that he had been compelled to accept de Caën's estimates, as under the terms of a decision of the Privy Council, he was bound to make them good. The king had promised to reimburse de Caën for his losses by payment of fourteen thousand three hundred and thirty pounds, of which eight thousand two hundred and seventy pounds were for his peltry and goods, and six thousand and sixty pounds for the vessels which had been captured. David Kirke strongly opposed the payment of this sum on the ground that it was excessive, but the king through his councillors ordered the payment to be made.

Having determined to seize the peltry brought to London from Quebec, the Kirke associates blew off the padlock which had been fixed to the storehouse door by an order of justice. Some time after, when Guillaume de Caën visited the store, accompanied by a member of the company and a constable, he discovered that only three hundred beaver skins and four hundred elk skins remained. Complaint was lodged with the king, who ordered Kirke to return the skins which were missing within three days, on pain of imprisonment or the confiscation of his property. None of the associates of Kirke appear to have obtained the sympathy of the public in that affair.

The English company had suffered a great loss over the transaction, and the king thought that it would be just to grant them some compensation. He therefore appointed two commissioners, Sir Isaac Wake and Burlamachi, to look after the interests of the English company. Their mission was to make an agreement with Guillaume de Caën, who represented the French company. After the exchange of

AN UNSATISFACTORY AGREEMENT

a long correspondence, the king of France agreed to pay to David Kirke the sum of twenty thousand pounds, on the condition that he should restore the fort of Quebec, the contents of the storehouse, the vessel belonging to Emery de Caën, and the peltry seized in Canada.

David Kirke was much dissatisfied with the agreement, which he believed was due to the action of Sir Isaac Wake, to whom he wrote, accusing him of not having followed the instructions of the English company. His letter concluded with these words: "I understand that the conduct of this affair has been absolutely irregular, as it is evident that you have only resorted to the French testimony, having no care for the English evidence."

In the same memorandum the Kirke family complained of the fact that the Company of English Adventurers had been compelled to plead in France, while the French were not subject to the same conditions. This accusation was not correct, as Guillaume de Caën had been obliged not only to live in London in order to vindicate his goods, but also to watch them and prevent damage.

Kirke had no other claim than compensation for losses, and de Caën, who had apparently no responsibility for the conflict of 1629, could not reasonably be expected to pay the amount of Kirke's claim. The contents of the storehouse at Quebec were the property of the de Caëns, and in visiting Quebec Emery de Caën had no other object in view than to secure his goods and take them to France. He had nothing to do with the war, and believed that he was sailing in times of peace. Thomas Kirke, by whom he was taken prisoner, treated him as a pirate, illegally, and in spite of the Treaty of Susa. It is true that the Kirkes were ignorant of this treaty when they sailed for America, but this was only an excuse for their attitude as belligerents.

As soon as the provisions of the negotiations were determined upon between the two countries, the claims had to be sent to the king, if the Kirkes considered that they had any grievance under the privileges conferred upon them by letters of marque. The royal commission took a correct stand in demanding from them in the name of Charles I an indemnity for France. All these differences were at length terminated through the energetic interference of Richelieu. These disputes had lasted for more than two years, and constantly occupied the attention of the ambassadors. The king of France, therefore, empowered Bullion and Bouthillier on January 25th, 1632, to act. Charles I had already sent Burlamachi to France with letters in favour of the restoration of Canada and Acadia, and had also given instructions to Sir Isaac Wake, his ambassador extraordinary. On March 5th, Louis XIII granted an audience to the ambassadors, and the basis of a treaty was agreed upon. Sir Isaac Wake represented Charles I, and Bullion and Bouthillier represented the king of France.

THE BASIS OF A TREATY

The commissioners took up the question of seizures, which was the most difficult. The king of France agreed to pay the sum of sixty-four thousand two hundred and forty-six pounds to Lumagne and Vanelly for the goods seized on the *Jacques*, and sixty-nine thousand eight hundred and sixty-six pounds for the goods seized on the *Bénédiction*, and to restore these two vessels to their owners within fifteen days. This agreement included the effects taken from the *Bride*, and sold at Calais, the property of Lumagne and Vanelly. The king of England promised to render and restore all the places occupied by the subjects of His Majesty of Great Britain in New France, Canada and Acadia, and to enjoin all those who commanded at Port Royal, at the fort of Quebec and at Cape Breton, to put these places in the hands of those whom it should please His Majesty, eight days after notice given to the officers named by the king of France.

Under this agreement, de Caën was obliged to pay for the equipment of a vessel of two hundred to two hundred and fifty tons, for the repatriation of the English subjects established in New France. The forts and places occupied by the English were to be restored as they were before their capture, with all arms and ammunition, according to the detailed list which Champlain had given. Burlamachi was authorized to pay for everything that was missing, and also to place Emery de Caën in possession of the ship *Hélène*, which had been taken from him, together with all goods abandoned at Quebec during his voyage of 1631. Burlamachi was also instructed to pay to Guillaume de Caën the sum of eighty-two thousand seven hundred livres within two months. The sum of sixty thousand six hundred and two livres tournois was also to be paid by Burlamachi to whomever it might belong, for the vessels *Gabriel* of St. Gilles, *Sainte-Anne*, of Havre de Grâce, *Trinité*, of Sables d'Olonne, *St. Laurent*, of St. Malo, and *Cap du Ciel*, of Calais, seized by the English after the signing of the Treaty of Susa.

After this was agreed to, the commissioners embodied in eight articles the conditions of trade between the two countries. The whole was signed by Wake, Bullion and Bouthillier, at St. Germain-en-Laye, on March 29th, 1632.

Thus terminated this quarrel between England and France, but it was only the precursor of a far more serious conflict which was to arise. From time to time, however, these differences were adjusted temporarily by treaties, only to lead to further complications. The principal difficulty arose regarding the boundaries of New France, the limits of which were not clearly defined in the treaty. Some adjacent parts were claimed by the English as their territory. The king of France had granted to the Hundred Associates "in all property, justice and seigniory, the fort and habitation of Quebec, together with the country of New France, or

GRANTS OF LAND

Canada, along the coasts . . . coasting along the sea to the Arctic circle for latitude, and from the Island of Newfoundland for longitude, going to the west to the great lake called Mer Douce (Lake Huron), and farther within the lands and along the rivers which passed through them and emptied in the river called St. Lawrence, otherwise the great river of Canada, etc."

Quebec was considered as the centre of these immense possessions of the king of France, which included the islands of Newfoundland, Cape Breton and St. John (Prince Edward).

The king of England had granted to Sir Thomas Gates and others, in 1606, three years after the date of de Monts' letters patent, "this part of America commonly called Virginia, and the territories between the thirty-fourth and forty-fifth degrees of latitude, and the islands situated within a space of one hundred miles from the coasts of the said countries."

In the year 1621, James I granted to Sir William Alexander, of Stirling, certain territory, which under the name of Nova Scotia was intended to comprise the present provinces of Nova Scotia, New Brunswick, the islands of St. John and Cape Breton, and the whole of Gaspesia. Charles I granted to Sir William Alexander in the year 1625 another charter, which ratified the one of 1621.

It is evident that the king of England and the king of France had each given charters covering

CHAMPLAIN

about the same extent of territory, and it is therefore easy to understand that tedious correspondence of a complicated nature thereby arose between the two countries. The treaty of St. Germain-en-Laye did not determine the question of the boundaries of the territory, and each power reserved its rights in this respect.

The inhabitants of Quebec at this time were in a state of suspense, for they had no knowledge of the progress made with the negotiations between the two countries. They had no reason to complain of the English, however, who treated them well, but the Huguenots, their own countrymen, who seemed prepared to serve under the English flag, were, as usual, troublesome and fanatical on religious questions. The settlers were so much distressed at not having the benefit of the ministration of a priest of their church, that they had resolved to leave the country at the earliest opportunity.

The Lutheran minister, who had decided to remain at Quebec with Kirke's men, had much to suffer. His advice was not accepted by his own people, and he was, moreover, kept in prison for a period of six months under the pretext of inciting the soldiers of the garrison to rebellion. All these disagreements rendered the condition of the Catholics almost unendurable.

On July 13th, 1632, a white flag was seen floating from a vessel which was entering the harbour of Quebec. The inhabitants were rejoiced, and when

THE RÉCOLLETS LEAVE CANADA

they were able to hear mass in the house of Madame Hébert, their happiness was complete. It was three years since they had enjoyed this privilege. One girl had been born in the interval, to the wife of Guillaume Couillard. But no death had been recorded, except the murder of an Iroquois prisoner by a Montagnais while in a state of intoxication.

The Jesuits who had arrived at the same time as Emery de Caën, took charge of the Quebec mission. In the year 1627, the Récollets, seeing that their mission had not apparently produced the results that they desired, and that they were also reduced to great distress, resolved to abandon New France for a country less ungrateful. We have seen that after the capitulation, the Récollets left with the greater number of the French for their motherland, but when they heard that Canada had been restored to France, they made preparations to resume their labours. Their superiors offered no objection, but the chief directors of the Hundred Associates, thinking the establishment of two different religious orders in the country, which as yet had no bishop, would create jealousies, determined to refuse the services of the Récollets.

Jean de Lauzon, intendant of the company for Canadian affairs, made a formal protest, and thus these noble missionaries were forced to abandon their work in Canada. The Récollets were much disappointed, but Father Le Caron, the first apostle to the Huron tribes, was so distressed at the news

CHAMPLAIN

that he was taken ill and died on March 29th, 1632, some days before the departure of Emery de Caën for Quebec. He had brought some manuscripts from Canada, which were accidently burnt in Normandy. This man was perhaps the purest example of all the Récollets in Canada. Others had a more illustrious name, but none gave greater proof of devotedness and courage in their dealings with the Indians, and especially the Hurons. He was generally regarded as a saint.

CHAPTER XIII

THE JESUIT MISSIONS IN NEW FRANCE

THE Jesuits, who had only been in the country about four years, had not as yet a true idea of the magnitude of the task they had undertaken. Father Charles Lalemant had abandoned the theatre of his first apostolic labours on our Canadian soil, at the same time that some workmen whom Father Noyrot had brought from France during the preceeding year, left the place. He was the last representative, together with Fathers Massé, de Noüe and de Brébeuf of the primitive church of Canada. Mention has been made of the temporary residence in the convent of the Récollets, and of a building which was erected for themselves at about two hundred feet from the shore, near the junction of the river Lairet and the river St. Charles. The Jesuits received a concession of this land which was bounded on the west by a stream called St. Michel, and the river St. Mary or Beauport on the east. This was named the Seigniory of Notre Dame des Anges.

The Jesuits' convent was finished on April 6th, 1626. It was a poor residence of about forty feet in length and thirty feet in width. The building contained a small chapel dedicated to Notre Dame des Anges, on account of a picture which decorated

CHAMPLAIN

a wall representing the Blessed Virgin receiving the homage of angels. This name extended beyond the chapel, and was given to the seigniory, and after a lapse of three centuries, it remains unchanged.

The different mission stations of the Jesuits in Canada and around the gulf of the St. Lawrence were maintained at the expense of the Hundred Associates from the year 1632, with the exception of their college at Quebec which was founded through the liberality of the Marquis de Gamache, who gave them a sum of sixteen thousand écus d'or for that purpose, in 1626, on the occasion of his son taking religious vows. The offer was accepted by Father Vitelleschi, general of the order, and the college was founded in 1635, and opened a few years later. "This," writes Parkman, "was the cradle of the great missions of Canada!"

As soon as the Jesuits arrived they commenced to repair their residence, and in a short time it was in a fit state for a banquet which was given to Emery de Caën, who had been appointed governor *ad interim* of the French colony.

Champlain returned from France to Quebec in the month of May of the following year, and again took over the government of New France. He brought with him Fathers Massé and Jean de Brébeuf, and their arrival was the dawn of a brighter era for the Canadian missions. The Jesuits founded, during the same year, a mission at Three Rivers, and another at Ihonatiria in the Huron country.

NOTRE DAME DES ANGES

The mission-stations at Miscou and at Cape Breton were also opened at about the same time, but they were all, practically speaking, dependent upon the liberality of the Hundred Associates.

The Jesuits in their Relations of 1635 regarded the establishment of the mission of Notre Dame des Anges as destined to fulfil three designs which they had in view for the honour and glory of God. These were: (1.) To erect a college for the education of young Frenchmen who were becoming more and more numerous. (2.) To found a seminary for young Indians for the purpose of civilizing or improving their moral condition. (3.) To extend the missions of the Jesuits among the Hurons and other savage tribes. These three designs were in a measure accomplished by this means. From the year 1626 Quebec was the principal centre of Canadian missions, which extended from Tadousac to the Great Lakes. Seeing that the French were all gathering in the vicinity of Fort St. Louis, and that their convent was exposed to attacks of the Indians, the Jesuits decided to build their new college upon the promontory of Cape Diamond. In the year 1637 the Hundred Associates conceded twelve acres of land to the Jesuits near Fort St. Louis, upon which they built their college and a church, some years after. The seminary for young Indians was opened in the year 1627, and Father Charles Lalemant conducted a class for them as long as there were pupils to attend.

CHAMPLAIN

The seminary of Notre Dame des Anges has an interesting though brief history. It was Father Le Jeune's intention to have removed it near to the fort. The question of transferring it to the Huron country, in order to obtain a greater number of pupils had been discussed, but there were many reasons against the change, the principal being that the proximity to the Huron families would have caused the fathers annoyance. The seminary was, therefore, continued at Notre Dame des Anges, where it remained until it was closed. Father Le Jeune wrote to the Provincial in France on August 28th, 1636:—

"I consider it very probable that, if we had a good building in Kébec we would get more children through the very same means by which we despaired of getting them. We have always thought that the excessive love the savages bear their children would prevent our obtaining them. It will be through this very means that they will become our pupils; for, by having a few settled ones, who will attract and retain the others, the parents, who do not know what it is to refuse their children, will let them come without opposition. And, as they will be permitted during the first few years to have a great deal of liberty, they will become so accustomed to our food and our clothes that they will have a horror of the savages and their filth. We have seen this exemplified in all the children brought up among our French. They get so well

FATHER LE JEUNE'S LETTER

acquainted with each other in their childish plays that they do not look at the savages, except to flee from them or make sport of them. Our great difficulty is to get a building, and to find the means with which to support these children. It is true we are able to maintain them at Notre Dame des Anges ; but as this place is isolated, so that there are no French children there, we have changed the plan that we formerly had to locate the seminary there. Experience shows us that it must be established where the bulk of the French population is, to attract the little savages by the French children. And, since a worthy and virtuous person has commenced by giving something for a seminary we are going to give up our attempts to clear some land, and shall make an effort to build at Kébec. I say an effort, for it is with incredible expense and labour that we build in these beginnings. What a blessing from God if we can write next year that instruction is being given in New France in three or four languages. I hope, if we succeed in getting a lodging, to see three classes at Kébec—the first, of little French children, of whom there will be perhaps twenty or thirty pupils ; the second, of Hurons ; the third, of Montagnés."

Father Daniel was the chief of the seminary, although he was generally assisted by other fathers, who instructed the children of the families residing near the convent. The chapel was used as a classroom, and both the boys and girls made good pro-

CHAMPLAIN

gress. They were soon taught to observe the customs of the French, such as joining their hands in prayers, kneeling or standing during the recitation of their lessons. They were also taught to answer with modesty, and to be respectful in their behaviour. The girls were especially apt at learning, and they endeavoured to imitate the French girls, for whom they appeared to have great love. At certain intervals a public meeting was held, at which the governor and the citizens of Quebec were present, and the pupils were questioned on religious subjects. The most successful received a reward at the hands of the governor, consisting of either a knife or an awl. They were called upon to kiss the governor's hand, and to make a bow *à la française.*

The pupils of the seminary were chiefly Hurons, and the names of some of the more prominent are known. These were Satouta, Tsiko, Teouatirhon, Andehoua, Aïandacé. The three first died during their residence in Quebec, on account of the change of air and of diet. Father Le Jeune has written that these young Indians were the columns of the seminary. They were, in fact, endued with many good qualities, and had given great hopes for the future. Satouta was the son of a Huron admiral, who was the most popular and best known Indian in the country. His authority was considered supreme, and in nautical matters his word was law. He had promised that at his death Satouta should inherit his name.

CLOSING OF THE SEMINARIES

Tsiko was the son of Ouanda Koka, one of the best speakers of his tribe, and he had won the esteem and admiration of his people through his talents. Tsiko had inherited his father's gifts, and spoke so well that he astonished all who heard him, especially the fathers.

Andehoua was a model of virtue. He was baptized under the name of Armand Jean, in honour of Cardinal Richelieu. The governor stood as his godfather. Andehoua made such good progress in his studies that he became a sort of missionary, and he did everything in his power to convert his countrymen. He died at the Hôtel Dieu, Quebec, in 1654, at the early age of thirty-six.

From the year 1639 the number of seminarists began to decrease, until there was only one. However, in the year 1643 four young Hurons went down to Quebec to receive instruction, and were baptized. Their godfathers were LeSueur de St. Sauveur, a priest, Martial Piraube, M. de Repentigny and M. de la Vallée. In the Relations of the Jesuits the names of three are preserved: Ateiachias, Atarohiat, and Atokouchioüani.

The seminary was then finally closed. The Jesuits opened another at Three Rivers, and at the commencement there were six pupils, but at the end of a year there were none. After eight years' experience, the Jesuits realized that it was impossible successfully to make an Indian boy adopt the manners and habits of the French, and the same result

CHAMPLAIN

was afterwards found by others who tried the experiment.

In the year 1635, the Jesuits' missions in New France included those at Cape Breton, Richibucto and Miscou Island. The mission of Miscou was the best organized and the most populous; the Catholics of Gaspé, Miramichi and Nipisiguit (Bathurst) went there. The island of Miscou is situated at the northern extremity of the coast of New Brunswick, near the entrance of the Baie des Chaleurs. It was the common residence of the Jesuits and of the two first who came here, Father Charles Turgis and Father Charles du Marché. On their arrival they found twenty-three Frenchmen there, who were endeavouring to form a settlement. Unfortunately, most of them were taken ill with scurvy, from which they died, including the captain, the surgeon, a clerk and nine or ten officers. Father du Marché was forced to leave the island, and finally Father Turgis succumbed to the disease, and left behind him a single man, who was in a dying condition.

In the year 1637, two other Jesuits came to this inhospitable island, Father Jacques de la Place and Father Nicholas Gondoin. They found only nine persons there, who were in charge of the storehouse. A year later, Father Claude Quentin, superior of the Canadian missions, came to assist his confrère, who had undertaken to erect a chapel, but after three years of constant labour, they both returned to Quebec in an exhausted condition.

FATHER DE LYONNE'S MISSIONS

Father Dollebeau and Father André Richard then took charge of the mission on the island of Miscou, but the former was taken ill and was obliged to return to France. During the voyage the vessel was captured by three English frigates, and while pillaging the ship a soldier set fire to the powder magazine, and as a result Father Dollebeau and the whole crew perished.

In the course of years, however, the Miscou mission increased, and the chapel proving insufficient to accommodate the congregation, the Jesuits built another at the entrance of the river Nipisiguit.

Father de Lyonne was the real founder of this new mission. Nipisiguit was a good trading and fishing-station, and a general rendezvous for the French as well as the Indians; it was also a safe harbour. Between the years 1650 and 1657, Father de Lyonne crossed the ocean three times in the interest of his mission, and in the year 1657 he founded another mission at Chedabucto, where he ended his career.

The field of the missionaries was divided after the year 1650. Father de Lyonne took charge of the mission at Chedabucto, while the stations at Miscou and Nipisiguit were under the control of Father Richard, and Father Frémin was given charge of the Richibucto mission. In the year 1661, Father Richard replaced Father de Lyonne at Chedabucto, but he only remained there one year.

CHAMPLAIN

The missions of the Jesuits in Acadia and Baie des Chaleurs closed with the departure of Father Richard. Some historians of Acadia mention the labours of Father Joseph Aubéri, whom Chateaubriand has immortalized in his "Atala." Father Aubéri prepared a map of Acadia, and also a memorandum of the boundaries of New France and New England in the year 1720.

The mission-station at Cape Breton was commenced in 1634, and Father Julian Perrault, a Jesuit, took up his residence there and gave religious instruction to the Micmacs, whom he found very attentive. The Micmacs were a hardy race, of great stature. Some of the men who were upwards of eighty years of age had not a single white hair.

Champlain gave to Cape Breton the name of St. Lawrence Island. The name was originally given to the cape but it was afterwards applied to the island. Bras d'Or was called Bibeaudock by the Indians, and Louisburg was commonly known as Port aux Anglais. The Portuguese had formerly occupied the island, but they were forced to leave it on account of the temperature and other causes. Nicholas Denys, who had been obliged to abandon Chedabucto, in Acadia, came to the island and founded Fort St. Pierre, which was taken from him in the year 1654 by Emmanuel le Borgne de Belle Isle, and by one Guilbault, a merchant of La Rochelle. Denys then took up his residence, sometimes at Miscou, sometimes at Gaspé or at Nipisiguit. His

THE CAPE BRETON MISSION

son Charles Denys, Sieur de Fronsac, had settled on the shores of the river Miramichi.

The first Jesuits who were invited to take charge of the Cape Breton mission were Fathers Vimont and de Vieux-Pont, who had been brought out by Captain Daniel, who, it will be remembered, lost a great deal of time in attacking the fort which had been built on the river du Grand Cibou by Stuart. The two Jesuits and forty men were left here. The Jesuits, however, returned to France in 1630. Fathers Davost and Daniel were missionaries at Cape Breton in 1633, and when Champlain visited the place on May 5th of that year, he met the two Jesuits, who soon afterwards returned with him to Quebec.

Father Perrault resided at Cape Breton during the years 1634 and 1635, and Fathers Richard and d'Endemare came in the following year and took up their residence at Fort Ste. Anne in Grand Cibou Bay. This place had many advantages, as it was naturally fortified, and three thousand small vessels could anchor safely in the bay. The Jesuits remained at Cape Breton until the arrival of Bishop de Laval in 1659. These various missions which we have recorded, constitute the religious history of the islands and coasts of the gulf of St. Lawrence during the greater part of the seventeenth century, and they were all founded by Champlain or begun under his administration, and he certainly took an active interest in the evangelisation of the Micmacs.

CHAMPLAIN

In a memorandum addressed to the king, Champlain had set forth his intention to erect a church at Quebec, to be dedicated to the Redeemer. He was, however, unable to accomplish his design. He had also made a solemn promise to the Blessed Virgin, between the years 1629 and 1632, to erect a church in honour of Notre Dame de la Recouvrance, should Quebec be regained, and on his return to Quebec he set out to fulfill his obligation. The occasion was favourable, as the chapel near the habitation in the Lower Town had been completely ruined.

The chapel of Notre Dame de la Recouvrance was erected during the summer of 1633, and in the autumn of the same year the Jesuits said mass for the inhabitants within the building. The increase of the population and their religious zeal, within the two following years, induced Champlain to raise this humble chapel into a small church. The building was therefore enlarged, and from that date the services assumed a solemnity of character which had been unknown before. Grand mass was celebrated every Sunday by a Jesuit, and the inhabitants each in turn offered consecrated loaves. In the afternoon, after vespers, the catechism was explained by the fathers. The French were very regular in their attendance at these ceremonies, and also at the religious instructions.

Father Charles Lalemant was the first Jesuit who lived at the presbytery as a parish priest. His successor was Father Jean de Quen. Father Le

NOTRE DAME DE LA RECOUVRANCE

Jeune wrote at that time:—"As soon as we had been lodged near the church (Notre Dame de la Recouvrance) Father Lalemant who had just begun to live at the residence, at the same time initiated its solemnities; Father de Quen, has succeeded him with the same inclination for ceremony. I frankly confess that my heart melted the first time I assisted in this divine service, at the sight of our Frenchmen so greatly rejoicing to hear sung aloud and publicly the praises of the great God in the midst of a barbarous people, at the sight of little children speaking the Christian language in another world. . . . Monsieur Gand's zeal in exercising all his energies to cause our French to love these solemn and public devotions, seems to me very praiseworthy. But the regulations of Monsieur our governor, his very remarkable example, and the piety of the more prominent people, hold all in the line of duty."

When Champlain was on his deathbed he was aware that his promise had been fulfilled. Notre Dame de la Recouvrance was then a fine church, and it was due to his labours. By his last will he bequeathed to this church all his personal chattels, and three thousand livres in stock of the Company of New France, and nine hundred livres which he had invested in a private company founded by some associates, together with a sum of four hundred livres from his private purse. It was the whole fortune of the first governor of New France. This will was afterwards contested and annulled, and the church was only allowed to receive the sum of nine hundred livres, which had been realized from the sale of his personal property. This sum was devoted to the purchase of a pyx, a silver gilt chalice, and a basin and cruets.

Several gifts were made for the decoration of the church of Notre Dame de la Recouvrance. Duplessis-Bochart presented two pictures, one representing the Blessed Virgin, and the other the Holy Family. De Castillon, seignior of the Island of Orleans, offered four small pictures, one of St. Ignace de Loyola, of St. François Xavier, of St. Stanislas de Kostka, and of St. Louis de Gonzagne, and also a large engraving of Notre Dame. Champlain had also placed on one of the walls a painting which had been rescued from the shipwreck during Father Noyrot's voyage.

During the year after Champlain's death, the Jesuits consecrated the church of Notre Dame de la Recouvrance under the name of the Immaculate Conception, which from that date was the special patron of the parochial church of Quebec.

The inauguration of this patronage afforded an opportunity for public rejoicing. On December 7th, 1636, a flag was hoisted on the fort and the cannon were fired many times. On the 8th, the day observed by the church in honour of the Immaculate Conception, the citizens fired a salute from the muskets at dawn, and they all assisted at mass, and received the Holy Communion. Devotion to the Mother of

THE FIRE OF 1640

God soon became general among the people, who were characterized as moral and honest.

Notre Dame de la Recouvrance was burnt on June 14th, 1640. In a few hours the residence of the Jesuits, the parochial church, and the chapel of Champlain, where his bones had been placed, were destroyed. The Relation of 1640 gives a short description of the catastrophe : " A rather violent wind, the extreme drouth, the oily wood of the fir of which these buildings were constructed, kindled a fire so quick and violent that hardly anything could be done. All the vessels and the bells and chalices were melted; the stuffs some virtuous persons had sent to us to clothe a few seminarists, or poor savages, were consumed in this same sacrifice. Those truly royal garments that His Majesty had sent to our savages to be used in public functions, to honour the liberality of so great a king, were engulfed in this fiery wreck, which reduced us to the hospital, for we had to go and take lodgings in the hall of the poor, until monsieur, our governor, loaned us a house, and after being lodged therein, the hall of the sick had to be changed into a church." This conflagration was a great loss. The registers were burnt, and the Jesuits had to reproduce them from memory. The chief buildings of Quebec had disappeared, and it was seventeen years before a a new church was built.

CHAPTER XIV

THE GROWTH OF QUEBEC

A QUARTER of a century had elapsed since the founding of Quebec, and still it could scarcely be regarded as other than a village, while in some parts of New France colonization was absolutely null. Agriculture had received some attention in the vicinity of Quebec, but it was on such a small scale that it should be termed gardening rather than farming.

Charlevoix writes: "The fort of Quebec, surrounded by a few wretched houses and some sheds, two or three cabins on the island of Montreal, as many, perhaps, at Tadousac, and at some other points on the river St. Lawrence, to accommodate fishers and traders, a settlement begun at Three Rivers and the ruins of Port Royal, this was all that constituted New France—the sole fruit of the discoveries of Verrazano, Jacques Cartier, de Roberval, Champlain, of the great expenses of the Marquis de la Roche and de Monts, and of the industry of many Frenchmen, who might have built up a great colony had they been well directed."

The various companies, as we have seen, took no interest whatever in settling the country, their chief design being to carry on fur trade with the Indians.

CHAMPLAIN

Patriotism had no meaning for them, the all-absorbing question was money. This was not the case, however, with the company established by Cardinal Richelieu, whose desire was to christianize the savages, to found a powerful colony, and to secure for his king the possession of New France. The principal associates of this company were pious, patriotic and zealous men, who laboured to extend the power and influence of France throughout the vast continent of America for the honour and glory of God. There were among the associates a certain number of gentlemen and ecclesiastics, who, realizing their incapacity to transact the business of such an important undertaking, preferred to hand over the administration to merchants of Dieppe, Rouen and Paris, together with the advantages to be derived therefrom. A special association was consequently formed, composed of merchants who undertook the financial affairs of the settlement, such as paying the new governor, providing ammunition and provisions, and maintaining the forts; and if there were profits they were to be divided amongst the Hundred Associates. This association was formed before the departure of Champlain for Quebec in 1633. Its agents were a merchant of Rouen named Rosée, and Cheffault, a lawyer of Paris, who had a representative at Quebec.

As it was necessary for the Hundred Associates to appoint a governor of New France, they offered the position to Champlain, as he was universally

THE SPRING OF 1633

respected and known to be experienced and disinterested. Moreover he was well acquainted with the country, and on friendly terms with the savages. It is doubtful whether any one could have taken his place with better prospects of success. Champlain, moreover, desired to finish his work, and although there was much to accomplish, the future appeared more favourable than at any other time. The company had a large capital at its disposal, and this alone seemed to insure the success of the colony. Three ships were equipped for Quebec in the spring of 1633, the *St. Pierre*, one hundred and fifty tons burden, carrying twelve cannon; the *St. Jean*, one hundred and sixty tons, with ten cannon, and the *Don de Dieu*, eighty tons, with six cannon. The ships carried about two hundred persons, including two Jesuits, a number of sailors and settlers, and one woman and two girls. Provisions and ammunition were in abundance. When the fleet arrived in the St. Lawrence, Champlain saw a number of English trading vessels which were there contrary to the treaty of St. Germain-en-Laye. From this moment Champlain resolved to establish a fixed post for trading, both for the Indians as well as strangers. The island selected for this purpose by Champlain was situated in the river St. Lawrence, about ten leagues above Quebec, and was named Richelieu Island.

Champlain caused the island to be fortified as soon as possible, and surrounded it with a platform, upon which cannon were placed pointing in every

CHAMPLAIN

direction. Sentinels were placed on guard, and it would have been impossible for vessels to pass unobserved. The Indians were informed of this new plan, and in the autumn of the same year, the Nipissings and the Algonquins of the Iroquet came to this island for trading. The Hurons, however, came to Quebec, as they had heard from the Algonquins of Allumette Island that the French would take revenge for the murder of Étienne Brûlé. Champlain did not desire to punish them for the death of this traitor, and he therefore did his best to retain the friendship of the Indians, and entertained them at public feasts. He knew well that their fur trade was of great importance, and, moreover, he wanted them as allies in the event of an attack by the Iroquois, which might be expected at any time, as they were unreliable and always anxious for war. A league with the Hurons, Algonquins and Montagnais, with one hundred French, would, in the opinion of Champlain, be sufficient to protect the colony, and he wrote to that effect to the cardinal. This was probably his last letter to the great minister:—

" MONSEIGNEUR :—The honour of the commands that I have received from your Eminence has inspired me with greater courage to render you every possible service with all the fidelity and affection that can be desired from a faithful servant. I shall spare neither my blood nor my life whenever the occasion shall demand them.

HIS LETTER TO RICHELIEU

"There are subjects enough in these regions, if your Eminence, considering the character of the country, shall desire to extend your authority over them. This territory is more than fifteen hundred leagues in length, lying between the same parallels of latitude as our own France. It is watered by one of the finest rivers in the world, into which empty many tributaries more than four hundred leagues in length, beautifying a country inhabited by a vast number of tribes. Some of them are sedentary in their mode of life, possessing, like the Muscovites, towns and villages built of wood; others are nomadic hunters and fishermen, all longing to welcome the French and religious fathers, that they may be instructed in our faith.

"The excellence of this country cannot be too highly estimated or praised, both as to the richness of the soil, the diversity of the timber such as we have in France, the abundance of wild animals, game and fish, which are of extraordinary magnitude. All this invites you, monseigneur, and makes it seem as if God had created you above all your predecessors to do a work here more pleasing to Him than any that has yet been accomplished.

" For thirty years I have frequented this country, and have acquired a thorough knowledge of it, obtained from my own observation and the information given me by the native inhabitants. Monseigneur, I pray you to pardon my zeal, if I say that, after your renown has spread throughout the

CHAMPLAIN

East, you should end by compelling its recognition in the West.

" Expelling the English from Quebec has been a very important beginning, but, nevertheless, since the treaty of peace between the two crowns, they have returned to carry on trade and annoy us in this river, declaring that it was enjoined upon them to withdraw, but not to remain away, and that they have their king's permission to come for the period of thirty years. But, if your Eminence wills, you can make them feel the power of your authority. This can furthermore be extended at your pleasure to him who has come here to bring about a general peace among these people, who are at war with a nation holding more than four hundred leagues in subjection, and who prevent the free use of the rivers and highways. If this peace were made, we should be in complete and easy enjoyment of our possessions. Once established in the country, we could expel our enemies, both English and Flemings, forcing them to withdraw to the coast, and, by depriving them of trade with the Iroquois, oblige them to abandon the country entirely. It requires but one hundred and twenty men, light armed for avoiding arrows, by whose aid, together with two or three thousand savage warriors, our allies, we should be, within a year, absolute masters of all these people ; and by establishing order among them, promote religious worship and secure an incredible amount of traffic.

THE HURON COUNTRY

"The country is rich in mines of copper, iron, steel, brass, silver, and other minerals which may be found here.

"The cost, monseigneur, of one hundred and twenty men is a trifling one to His Majesty, the enterprise the most noble that can be imagined.

"All for the glory of God, whom I pray with my whole heart to grant you ever increasing prosperity, and to make me all my life, monseigneur, your most humble, most faithful and most obedient servant, "CHAMPLAIN.
"At Quebec, in New France, August 15th, 1635."

In order to consolidate his general scheme for the colonization of the country, Champlain desired that the missionaries should settle permanently among the Huron tribes. The Jesuits wished to go there, as they believed they would find a field for their labours. They had previously set before the people the light of the Catholic faith, but these efforts had not been as successful as they had wished. Father de Brébeuf, the apostle to the Hurons, having decided to return to his former sphere of labours, left for the Huron country in 1634, prepared to remain there as long as there was work to be done. He was destined to live among the Hurons until they were finally dispersed by the Iroquois.

When Champlain arrived at Quebec, he summoned Emery de Caën to deliver to Duplessis-Bochart the keys of the fort and habitation. Champlain's arrival caused much rejoicing among the

CHAMPLAIN

inhabitants, for he inspired both their love and respect, and he was, perhaps, the only man who could impress them with a belief in their future, and thus retain them in the country. The arrival of a certain number of settlers during the years 1633-4, was also an encouragement for all. The restoration of Canada to France caused some excitement in the maritime provinces of France, especially in Normandy, as most of the settlers of New France up to this date were from there. The exceptions were, Louis Hébert, a native of Paris, and Guillaume Couillard, of St. Malo. Emigration soon extended to other parts of the provinces, as the result of the publication of the Relations of the Jesuits, which had been issued in Paris and elsewhere during the years 1632 and 1633. Several pious and charitable persons began to take an interest in the missions of New France, and forwarded both money and goods to help them.

Some nuns offered to go to Canada to look after the sick and to instruct the young girls, and in the year 1633 a few families arrived in Quebec with Champlain, who had defrayed their expenses.

In the year 1634 an association was formed in France for the purpose of promoting colonization, and a group of about forty persons, recruited in different parts of the province of Perche, were sent to Canada, with Robert Giffard at their head. Giffard, it will be remembered, had visited Quebec in the year 1627 as surgeon of the vessels sent out by

ROBERT GIFFARD

the company, but he had no intention of settling in the country. After having built a log hut on the Beauport shore, he devoted his leisure to hunting and fishing, game and fish being plentiful at that time, and returned to France during the same year. He was appointed surgeon to Roquemont's fleet during the following year, and as the vessels were captured by the English, he, with the others on board, was compelled to return to his mother country. This misfortune did not discourage the former solitary inhabitant of Beauport, and he resolved to revisit the country, but this time with a view of settling and of farming.

Giffard had suffered many losses, and as a compensation for his services and misfortune, he obtained a tract of land from the Company of New France, one league in length and a league and a half in breadth, situated between the rivers Montmorency and Beauport, bounded in front by the river St. Lawrence, and in the rear by the Laurentian Mountains. He was also granted as a special favour, a tract of land of two acres in extent, situated near the fort, for the purpose of building a residence, surrounded with grounds. These concessions, which seem large at first sight, were, however, not new to the colony. Louis Hébert had been granted the fief of the Sault au Matelot, and the fief Lepinay, while the Jesuits had received the fief of Notre Dame des Anges almost free of conditions.

CHAMPLAIN

Under these favourable conditions Giffard induced two citizens of Mortagne, Zacharie Cloutier and Jean Guyon, to accompany him to Canada. Cloutier was a joiner, and Guyon a mason. They promised their seignior that they would build him a residence, thirty feet long and sixteen feet wide.

The other emigrants came to Canada at their own risk. The party numbered forty-three persons, including women and children, and were within a space of from five to eight leagues of Mortagne, the chief town of the old province of Perche. There were two exceptions, however, Jean Juchereau came from La Ferté Vidame in Thimerais, and Noël Langlois was from St. Leonard, in Normandy.

The vessels bearing the contingent of settlers arrived in Quebec in June. They were four in number, under the command of Captains de Nesle, de Lormel, Bontemps, and Duplessis-Bochart. Robert Giffard had preceded the party by a few days, and he lost no time in selecting the spot where his residence was to be built, upon which he planted a cross on July 25th. He also commenced clearing the land, and two years after he gathered in a harvest of wheat sufficient to maintain twenty persons. The soil in this part was very productive, and it is, even to-day, the richest in the province of Quebec.

Among the emigrants of the year 1634 were two remarkable men, Jean Bourdon, and a priest named Jean LeSueur de St. Sauveur. The Abbé LeSueur de St. Sauveur had abandoned his parish of St.

JEAN BOURDON

Sauveur de Thury, which is to-day known as Thury-Harcourt, in Normandy, to come to Quebec. One of the suburbs of Quebec to-day takes its name from this active and devoted priest.

Jean Bourdon, an inseparable friend of the abbé, established himself on the borders of Côteau Ste. Geneviève, which is to-day known as St. John's suburb. He built a house and a mill, and also a chapel, which he named Chapel St. Jean. Other pioneers soon settled near Bourdon's place, which finally gave to Quebec a suburb.

Bourdon was a man of great capacity, and he in turn filled the rôle of surveyor, engineer, cartographer, delineator, farmer, diplomat and lawyer. He saw the colony increasing, and knew eight governors of the colony, including Champlain. He was also acquainted with Bishop Laval, the Venerable Mother Marie Guyart de l'Incarnation, and was on good terms with the Jesuits and the nuns of the Hôtel Dieu and Ursuline Convent. Bourdon played an important part in the affairs of the colony. He was present at the foundation of the Jesuits' college, of the Quebec seminary, and of the Conseil Souverain, of which he was procureur fiscal. Of his personal qualities, the Venerable Mother de l'Incarnation has written that he was "the father of the poor, the comfort of orphans and widows, a good example for everybody."

One of the articles of the act incorporating the Company of New France, provided that the colony

CHAMPLAIN

was to be settled with French and Catholic subjects only. This provision may appear at first sight to be arbitrary, but when we consider that one of the chief objects of the colonization of New France was to convert the savages, and that the Huguenots with their new form of religion were, generally speaking, hostile to the king and to the Catholics, it seems to have been a judicious provision. In such a small community the existence of two creeds so opposed to each other could hardly have produced harmony, and as the Catholics were undertaking the enterprise and it originated with them, they surely had the right to do what they considered would most effectively secure their ends.

For political reasons this action could also be defended, for the loyalty of the Huguenots was, perhaps, doubtful, and their past actions did not offer any guarantee for the future. They did not hesitate to preach revolt against the authorities of France, and, therefore, intimate connection with the Indians might have produced results prejudicial to the colony. If France had the welfare of the colony at heart, it behooved her to exclude every disturbing element. Viewed impartially, this precaution was undoubtedly just, and those who blame the company for their action, do not rightly understand the difficulties which existed at that period.

Richelieu, who had a clear insight into the affairs of the time, did not prohibit trade between the Huguenots and the Indians, but he refused them

A RELIGIOUS BASIS

permission to settle in Canada, or to remain there for any length of time without special leave. Champlain had observed the attitude of the Huguenots, their unwillingness to erect a fort at Quebec, their clashes with the Catholics, and their treatment of the Jesuits, and although he was not fanatical, he was pleased with this rule. The foundation of the new settlement was based upon religion, and religion was essential to its progress. Peace and harmony must be maintained, and everything that would promote trouble or quarrel must be excluded.

During the seventeenth century, England pursued a hostile policy towards Catholics. A Catholic was not eligible for a public office, and the learned professions were closed to them, neither could a Catholic act as a tutor or as an executor to a will. Prejudice was carried still further, and even the books treating of their faith were suppressed, while relics or religious pictures were forbidden. These were only a few of the persecutions to which they were subject.

In 1621 Champlain had joined in a request to the king to forbid Protestant emigration to Canada, but his petition was not granted, because the company was composed of mixed creeds. The company formed by Richelieu, however, was solely Catholic, and there were no difficulties on this score. The result of this policy was soon manifest. There were no more dissensions on board the vessels as to places of worship, and the Catholics were, as a consequence, enabled to observe their religious duties without fear of annoyance. The beneficent influence of this policy extended to the settlement, where the people lived in peace, and were not subject to the petty quarrels which arose through a difference in creed.

In the Relation of 1637 we find evidence of this: "Now it seems to me that I can say with truth that the soil of New France is watered by so many heavenly blessings, that souls nourished in virtue find here their true element, and are, consequently, healthier than elsewhere. As for those whose vices have rendered them diseased, they not only do not grow worse, but very often, coming to breathe a salubrious air, and far removed from opportunities for sin, changing climate they change their lives, and a thousand times bless the sweet providence of God, which has made them find the door to felicity where others fear only misery.

"In a word, God has been worshipped in His houses, preaching has been well received, both at Kébec and at the Three Rivers, where Father Buteux usually instructed our French people; each of our brethren has been occupied in hearing many confessions, both ordinary and general; very few holidays and Sundays during the winter have passed in which we have not seen and received persons at the table of our Lord. And certain ones, who for three, four and five years had not confessed in old France, now, in the new, approach this so salutary

THE RELATION OF 1637

sacrament oftener than once a month; prayers are offered kneeling and in public, not only at the fort, but also in families and little companies scattered here and there. As we have taken for patroness of the Church of Kébec the Holy Virgin under the title of her Conception, which we believe to be immaculate, so we have celebrated this festival with solemnity and rejoicing.

"The festival of the glorious Patriarch Saint Joseph, father, patron and protector of New France, is one of the great solemnities of this country. . . . It is, in my opinion, through his favour and through his merits, that the inhabitants of New France who live upon the banks of the great river Saint Lawrence, have resolved to receive all the good customs of the old and to refuse admission to the bad ones.

"And to tell the truth, so long as we have a governor who is a friend of virtue, and so long as we have free speech in the Church of God, the monster of ambition will have no altar there.

"All the principal personages of our colony honour religion; I say with joy and God's blessing, that those whom His goodness has given to command over us, and those also who are coming to establish themselves in these countries, enjoy, cherish, and wish to follow the most sincere maxims of Christianity. . . . Justice reigns here, insolence is banished, and shamelessness would not dare to raise its head. . . . It is very important to introduce good laws and pious customs in these early beginnings,

CHAMPLAIN

for those who shall come after us will walk in our footsteps, and will readily conform to the example given them by us, whether tending to virtue or vice."

We could multiply evidence on this point. The Jesuits always recall this good feature of the settlers, their respect for their religion, its worship and its ministers.

The author of the "Secret Life of Louis XV," says that New France owed its vigour to its first settlers; their families had multiplied and formed a people, healthy, strong, honourable, and attached to good principles. Father Le Clercq, a Récollet, the Venerable Mother de l'Incarnation, and many others, seem to take pleasure in praising the virtues of our first ancestors.

Champlain had begun his administration by establishing order everywhere, and chiefly among the soldiers, who easily understood military discipline, but the religious code with more difficulty. Fort St. Louis was like a school of religion and of every virtue. They lived there as in a monastery. There was a lecture during meals; in the morning they read history, and at supper the lives of saints. After that they said their prayers, and Champlain had introduced the old French custom of ringing the church bells three times a day, during the recitation of the Angelus. At night, every one was invited to go to Champlain's room for the night's prayer, said by Champlain himself.

AN HONOURABLE CAREER

These good examples, given by Champlain, governor of the country, were followed, and produced good fruits of salvation among the whole population. The blessing of God on the young colony was evident, and when Champlain died, he had the consolation of leaving after him a moral, honest and virtuous people.

CHAPTER XV

CONCLUSION

IN the autumn of the year 1635, Champlain suffered from a stroke of paralysis, which was considered very severe from the commencement. However, hopes were entertained for his recovery. The months of October and November passed away, and still no sign of improvement appeared. Champlain, therefore, made his will, which he was able to sign plainly, in the presence of some witnesses. Father Charles Lalemant, the friend and confessor of Champlain, administered to him the last rites of the church, and on the night of December 25th, 1635, he passed away at Fort St. Louis.

All the inhabitants, without exception, were deeply affected on hearing the news of his demise, and a great number attended his funeral. The funeral sermon was preached by Father Le Jeune. Champlain was buried in a grave which had been specially prepared, and later on, a small chapel was erected to protect his precious remains.[1] This chapel was

[1] The exact site of the chapel wherein Champlain was buried is unknown, although many antiquarians have endeavoured to throw light upon the subject. In 1866 some bones and the fragment of an inscription were found in a kind of vault at the foot of Breakneck Stairs, and Messrs. Laverdière and Casgrain were under the impression that Champlain's tomb had been found. In 1875 the Abbé Casgrain discovered a

CHAMPLAIN

unfortunately burnt, as we have already mentioned, during the conflagration of June 14th, 1640.

The Jesuits' Relations of 1636 give a full account of the last days of Champlain, which we here quote: " On December 25th, the day of the birth of our Saviour upon earth, Monsieur de Champlain, our governor, was reborn in Heaven ; at least we can say that his death was full of blessings. I am sure that God has shown him this favour in consideration of the benefits he has procured for New France, where we hope some day God will be loved and served by our French, and known and adored by our savages. Truly he had led a life of great justice, equity and perfect loyalty to his king and towards the gentlemen of the company. But at his death he crowned his virtues with sentiments of piety so lofty that he astonished us all. What tears he shed ! How ardent became his zeal for the service of God ! How great was his love for the families here—saying that they must be vigorously assisted for the good of the country, and made comfortable in every possible way in these early stages, and that he would do it if God gave him health. He was not

document which he considered proved that the chapel had been built in the Upper Town, in the vicinity of the parochial church and of Fort St. Louis. This opinion was further confirmed by other documents which have since been found. The chapel was in existence in the year 1661, but after this date no mention is made of it. The parochial archives contain no mention of the place, and the only facts that we have concerning the tomb, are that Father Raymbault and Francois de Ré, Sieur Gand, were buried near Champlain's remains.

MADAME CHAMPLAIN

taken unawares in the account which he had to render unto God, for he had long ago prepared a general confession of his whole life, which he made with great contrition to Father Lalemant, whom he honoured with his friendship. The father comforted him throughout his sickness, which lasted two months and a half, and did not leave him until his death. He had a very honourable burial, the funeral procession being formed of the people, the soldiers, the captains and the churchmen. Father Lalemant officiated at this burial, and I was charged with the funeral oration, for which I did not lack material. Those whom he left behind have reason to be well satisfied with him; for although he died out of France, his name will not therefore be any less glorious to posterity."

Champlain left no posterity. His wife spent only four years in Canada, after which she resided continually in Paris. During her residence in New France, she studied the Algonquin language, and instructed the young Indians in catechism, and in this manner she won the friendship of the native tribes. It was the fashion of the time for a lady of quality to wear at her girdle a small mirror, and the youthful Hélène observed the custom. The savages, who were delighted to be in her company, were oft time astonished to see their own image reflected on the crystalline surface of this mirror, and said, with their native simplicity: " A lady so handsome, who cures our diseases, and loves us to so great an extent as to bear our image near her breast, must be superior to a human being." They, therefore, had a kind of veneration for her, and they would have offered their homage to her instead of to the Deity of whom they had only an imperfect knowledge.

The Indians were Madame Champlain's special care, but she was respected by the French as well. We do not know very much about her social intercourse with the different families of Quebec, but it is not probable that she ignored Madame Hébert or her family, as Faillon seems to believe. Her own distinction and the position of her husband would, no doubt, render her particular in the choice of friends, but we can scarcely believe that she would completely ignore Madame Couillard, who was of her own age. How was it that she consented to live alone in Quebec during the long absence of her husband?

After her return to Paris in 1624, Madame Champlain lived alone, and became more and more detached from the world, till she asked her husband to allow her to enter an Ursuline convent. Champlain, fearing that this desire might arise rather from caprice than a vocation for the life of the cloister, thought it advisable to refuse her request, and he bade her a last adieu in 1633. After Champlain's death, Father Le Jeune informed her that she was now free to follow the dictates of her heart.

According to the marriage settlement, Champlain

HIS WILL

was obliged to leave to his wife, if she were still living, all his possessions. By his last will, however, he left all his property to the church. Champlain had no desire to injure his wife by this act; on the contrary, he knew that her piety was great, and that she would probably applaud the course he had taken, which was owing to his extraordinary devotion to Notre Dame de la Recouvrance, the church which he had built and loved. Madame Champlain, in fact, made no opposition, and the will was confirmed on July 11th, 1637. The will, however, was contested by Marie Camaret, a first cousin of Champlain, and wife of Jacques Hersault, comptroller of customs at La Rochelle, and a famous trial was the result. The will was contested on two grounds: (1.) That the will was contrary to the marriage settlement, and therefore ought to be annulled; (2.) That the will was made by foreign hands, as it was difficult to suppose that Champlain had chosen the Virgin Mary as his heir.

These were the contentions of Master Boileau. The attorney-general Bignon easily refuted the second allegation by proving that Madame Champlain had recognized the signature of her husband, and had stated that the expression and style were his. The terms of this bequest to the Virgin were quite natural to a man of Champlain's character, "When we know," said the attorney, "that he frequently made use of Christian expressions in his general conversation."

CHAMPLAIN

Although the authenticity of the will was proved, the attorney-general argued that it ought to be set aside in face of the deed of settlement. The court upheld this view, and the property of Champlain, with the exception of the sum of nine hundred livres, derived from the sale of his chattels, returned to his natural heirs.

This trial and other affairs prevented Madame Champlain from carrying out her resolution, and it was not until November 7th, 1645, that she entered the monastery of St. Ursula at Paris. She first entered the institution as a benefactress, and soon after became a novice under the name of Hélène de St. Augustin. There seems to have been some difficulties with regard to her profession as a nun, and she therefore resolved to found an Ursuline monastery at Meaux. Bishop Séguier granted the necessary permission to found the monastery, and also for her to take with her three nuns and a lay sister. Hélène de St. Augustin left Paris for Meaux on March 17th, 1648, and made her profession five months after. As a preparation for this solemn act, she made a public confession in the presence of the community. She also recited her faults, kneeling, and wearing a cord about her neck, and bearing a lighted taper in her hands. Mère Hélène de St. Augustin lived only six years in her convent at Meaux, and died on December 20th, 1654, at the age of fifty years, leaving the memory of a saintly life.

A NOBLE CHARACTER

Eustache Boullé, the brother of Hélène de St. Augustin, became a convert to Catholicism through the intervention of his sister, and entered the Minim order. He was sent to Italy, where he lived for six years. During his sojourn there his sister sent to him one thousand livres a year, and. at her death she bequeathed to him the sum of six thousand livres, and all her chattels, together with a pension of four hundred livres for life.

All those who have carefully studied the life of Champlain, have been impressed by the many brilliant qualities which he possessed. Some have praised his energy, his courage, his loyalty, his disinterestedness, and his probity. Others have admired the charity which he exhibited towards his neighbours, his zeal, his practical faith, his exalted views and his perseverance. The fact is, that in Champlain all these qualities were united to a prominent degree.

The contemporaries of Champlain did not perhaps appreciate his merits, or his heroic efforts as a founder. This is not altogether singular, for even in the physical world one cannot rightly estimate the altitude of a mountain by remaining close to its base, but at a distance a just appreciation of its proportions may be obtained.

If the contemporaries of Champlain failed to render him justice, posterity has made amends, and Time, the sole arbitrator of fame, has placed the founder of Quebec upon a pedestal of glory which will become more brilliant as the centuries roll on.

CHAMPLAIN

Nearly three centuries had elapsed since the heroic Saintongeais first set foot on the soil of Canada, when, at the close of the nineteenth century, a spectacle was witnessed in the city of his foundation which proved that the name of Champlain was graven on the hearts of all Canadians. The ceremonies attending the inauguration of the splendid monument which now adorns Quebec, have become a matter of history, and seldom could such a scene be repeated again. France and England, the two great nations from which Canadians have descended, each paid homage to the illustrious founder; nor can we forget the noble tribute which was paid by the latest English governor, representing Her Majesty Queen Victoria, to the first French governor, representing His Majesty the King of France and of Navarre.

It is seldom that the deeds of the great men of past ages have been more fittingly remembered. Champlain, as we have previously remarked, possessed in an eminent degree all the qualities necessary for a founder, and his character is therefore exceptional, for over and above all the heroism he displayed, all his perseverance, his devotion to his country, we behold the working of a Christian mind, and the desire to propagate the faith of his fathers.

What would have been the result of the missions without his aid? It was Champlain who caused the Catholic standard to be planted on the shores of Canada. It was he who brought the missionaries to

THE FATHER OF NEW FRANCE

the new settlement, and maintained them at Quebec, at Tadousac, and in the Huron country. It was Champlain, too, who founded the parochial church of Quebec, and afterwards endowed it.

Champlain's work rested solely upon a religious foundation, hence his work has endured. It is true that the founder of Quebec had certain worldly ambitions: he desired to promote commerce between the French and the Indians, but surely this is not a matter for which he should be reproached. Without trade the inhabitants of the settlement could not exist, and without the development of the settlement, his work of civilization would necessarily end. He worked for the material prosperity of the settlement, but not to increase his own fortune. The development of trade was also essential to Champlain in his capacity of explorer, and it was only through this means that he could extend the bounds of his mother country. This was surely the wisdom of a true patriot. What nobler ambition on earth could any one have than this, to extend the kingdom of his God and of his king?

Champlain has been justly called *The Father of New France*, and this is certainly a glorious title. The name of Champlain is indissolubly associated with this country, and will live long after his contemporaries are forgotten, for many of them now only live through him.

America contains a number of towns which have carefully preserved the names of their founders,

CHAMPLAIN

whose memories are consecrated by monuments which will recall to future generations their noble work. But where is the town or state that can point to a founder whose work equalled that of Champlain? He had to spend thirty of the best years of his life in his endeavours to found a settlement on the shores of the St. Lawrence. Twenty times he crossed the Atlantic in the interests of the colony, and in the meantime he had constantly to combat the influence of the merchants who vigorously opposed the settlement of the French in Canada.

If we study the history of the mercantile companies from the years 1608 to 1627, we find on the one hand, a body of men absorbed by one idea, that of growing rich, and on the other hand, a man, anxious, it is true, to look after the material interests of the merchants and of the people, but hand in hand with this the desire to extend the dominion of his sovereign. Here was a vast country, capable of producing great wealth, and struggling for its possession was a body of avaricious men, while valiantly guarding its infancy, we find a single champion, the heroic Champlain. Champlain watched over the new settlement with the tender solicitude of a parent carefully protecting his offspring from danger, and ready to sacrifice his life to save it from disaster. In small vessels of sixty or eighty tons, Champlain had repeatedly exposed his life to danger in crossing the ocean. His health had also been exposed during the days and nights spent in the open forests, or when

PRUDENT AND CHARITABLE

passing on the dangerous rivers in his efforts to explore new territory. He was also constantly at the mercy of the Indians, whose treachery was proverbial. Under all these dangers and through all these conditions, Champlain's conduct was exemplary. He was charitable as a missionary towards these poor children of the woods. When threatened with hunger or malady, he relieved their wants and took care of the young children, some of whom he adopted. Others again he placed in French families, hoping that sooner or later they would be baptized into the fold of Christ's flock. In his intercourse with the chiefs, Champlain took occasion to explain to them the rudiments of the Christian faith, hoping thereby to pave the way for the work of the missionaries. Whenever he found any children that seemed more intelligent than usual, he sent them to France, where they could be instructed, and either enter a convent or take service in some good family. And who can tell whether some of these children did not afterwards become missionaries to their own country?

Champlain's prudence in his dealings with the savages was not less remarkable than his charity. This conduct gave him an influence over the Indians that no other Frenchman was able to obtain. The Indian tribes regarded Champlain as a father, but their love was mingled with a reverential fear, and every word and action was of deep significance to them. They had faith in Champlain, which after all was not unusual, for he had never deceived them. Though they were barbarous and uncouth, and generally untruthful, they could distinguish the false from the true from the lips of a Frenchman. Though given to dissimulation themselves, they could appreciate sincerity in others.

Some writers have questioned Champlain's prudence touching the alliance which he made with some Indians for the purpose of fighting the aggressive Iroquois. We have already shown that if Champlain desired to maintain his settlement at Quebec, such an alliance was not only prudent, but essential. The Hurons and allied tribes, it is true, were barbarous, though not to so great an extent as the Iroquois, but they had the same vices and were as perfidious. The least discontent or whim would have been sufficient for the whole band to have swept the fort away. By making an alliance with them, and promising to assist them against their inveterate foes, it became to their advantage to support Champlain, and thus to render his people secure against attack. Moreover the numerical strength of the settlers in the early days was not sufficient for Champlain to have imposed terms by force of arms, and as it was necessary for his people to trade with the Indians, he could not have done better, under the circumstances, than to form this alliance, which insured business relations and protection for his countrymen.

This alliance was undoubtedly made at a sacrifice

A CONCILIATORY POLICY

to Champlain, and he had to suffer many humiliations and privations thereby. We cannot imagine that he found any pleasure in going to war with a lot of savages, or in fighting against a ferocious band, with whom neither he nor his people had any quarrel. It is certain that Champlain did not encourage them in their wars, and he was careful not to put any weapons into their hands. The same amount of prudence was not exercised by those who came after the French and endeavoured to colonize New England and New Netherland.

Champlain's policy was one of conciliation. He desired peace, harmony and charity above all things. As a respectful and obedient child of his mother, the Catholic Church, he was very anxious that her teachings and advice should be observed by those who were placed under his authority. Although in his early life he had followed the career of a soldier, still he regarded the profession of arms as useful only to put into question the ancient axiom, *Si vis pacem, para bellum*. Wars and quarrels had no attraction for Champlain, and he always preferred a friendly arrangement of any difficulty. He was a lover of peace, rather than of bloodshed, and the kindly nature of his disposition prevented him adopting vigorous measures.

Nevertheless, in the fulfilment of his duty as a judge, he was just, and would punish the guilty in order to restrain abuses or crimes. At this period there was no court of justice in New France, but

CHAMPLAIN

Champlain's commission empowered him to name officers to settle quarrels and disputes. There was a king's attorney, a lieutenant of the Prévôté, and a clerk of the Quebec jurisdiction, which had been established by the king. Champlain, however, was often called upon to decide a point of law, and we learn from his history that he was unable on account of death to settle a point which had arisen between two of Robert Giffard's farmers.

Champlain's authority was very extended, and whatever good may have resulted from his administration is due to the fact that he exercised his power with wisdom and prudence. Champlain's influence has expanded throughout the country wherever the French language is spoken, from the Huron peninsula, along the Algonquins' river, from Sault St. Louis, Tadousac and Quebec, and every one has recognized that Champlain alone, among the men of his day, had sufficient patriotism and confidence in the future of the colony to maintain and hold aloft under great difficulties, the lily banner of France on our Canadian shores.

After having founded Quebec, Champlain, with characteristic wisdom, chose the places where now stand the cities of Montreal and Three Rivers. He was particularly fortunate in his selections, and any buildings that he caused to be erected, were built from his own plans and under his own directions.

On the whole, Champlain's writings are very interesting, notwithstanding the fact that he is

HIS WRITINGS

somewhat diffuse in his style. Writing in the style of the commencement of the seventeenth century, we see traces, especially in his figures and descriptions, of the beauties of a language which was then in a transitory state. However, whether his style may be commended or condemned, it is of little consequence, since he has given to the world such ample details of his life and achievements as a discoverer, an explorer and a founder. His writings are the more remarkable from the fact that they were composed during the scanty leisure of his daily life, and we owe him a debt of gratitude for having sacrificed this leisure to give us such precious treasures.[1] Such was the life of this peerless man, whose incessant labours were dedicated to the service of God and the glory of France.

The city of Quebec is justly proud of her noble founder, and it is a source of gratification to the inhabitants to point to the stately monument which stands upon the spot consecrated by the life and death of Champlain. The inscription commemorates the great work of the founder, and of his explorations; but in the hearts of the people of Canada, Champlain has a still more precious monument, and the flourishing condition of our Dominion to-day is

[1] The last publication of Champlain bears the date of 1632, with the following title: *Les Voyages de la Nouvelle France occidentale, dicte Canada, faits par le Sr. de Champlain Xainctongeois, Capitaine pour le Roy en la Marine du Ponant, et toutes les Descouvertes qu'il a faites en ce pays depuis l'an 1603, jusques en l'an 1629. MDCXXXII.* This volume is dedicated to Richelieu. According to M. Laverdière, it was reissued, in 1640, with a new date and title.

CHAMPLAIN

but the unconscious outcome of the trial and labours of his heroic life.

All historians who have written of Champlain attribute to him the qualities which we have endeavoured to depict in these pages. Charlevoix, a Jesuit, and the author of the first great history of Canada, written about one hundred years after the death of the founder of New France, thus writes:

"Champlain died at Quebec, generally and justly regretted. M. de Champlain was, beyond contradiction, a man of merit, and may be well called, *The Father of New France*. He had good sense, much penetration, very upright views, and no man was ever more skilled in adopting a course in the most complicated affairs. What all admired most in him was his constancy in following up his enterprises, his firmness in the greatest dangers, a courage proof against the most unforeseen reverses and disappointments, ardent and disinterested patriotism, a heart tender and compassionate for the unhappy, and more attentive to the interests of his friends than his own, a high sense of honour and great probity. His memoirs show that he was not ignorant of anything that one of his profession should know, and we find in him a faithful and sincere historian, an attentively observant traveller, a judicious writer, a good mathematician and an able mariner.

"But what crowns all these good qualities is the fact that in his life, as well as in his writings, he shows himself always a truly Christian man, zealous

CHARLEVOIX'S TRIBUTE

for the service of God, full of candour and religion. He was accustomed to say what we read in his memoirs, 'That the salvation of a single soul was worth more than the conquest of an empire, and that kings should seek to extend their domain in heathen countries only to subject them to Christ.' He thus spoke especially to silence those who, unduly prejudiced against Canada, asked what France would gain by settling it. Our kings, it is known, always spoke like Champlain on this point; and the conversion of the Indians was the chief motive which, more than once, prevented their abandoning a colony, the progress of which was so long retarded by our impatience, our inconstancy, and the blind cupidity of a few individuals. To give it a more solid foundation, it only required more respect for the suggestions of M. de Champlain, and more seasonable belief on the part of those who placed him in his position. The plan which he proposed was but too well justified by the failure of opposite maxims and conduct."

In 1880, the Reverend E. F. Slafter,[1] a Protestant

[1] Edmund Farwell Slafter was born in Norwich, Vt., on May 30th, 1816. He was graduated at Dartmouth in 1840, studied at Andover Theological Seminary, and in 1844 was ordained a minister of the Protestant Episcopal Church. Since 1877 he has given his leisure time to historical studies. He has published, among other works, *Sir William Alexander and American Colonization*, in the series of the Prince Society (Boston, 1873), *Voyages of the Northmen to America*, edited with an introduction (1877), *Voyages of Samuel de Champlain*, translated from the French by Charles Pomeroy Otis, with historical illustrations and a memoir (three volumes, 1878, 1880, 1882).

CHAMPLAIN

minister, gave to the American nation an appreciative description of the virtues of Champlain, from which we quote the following passage: "In completing this memoir the reader can hardly fail to be impressed, not to say disappointed, by the fact that results apparently insignificant should thus far have followed a life of able, honest, unselfish, heroic labour. The colony was still small in numbers, the acres subdued and brought into cultivation were few, and the aggregate yearly products were meagre. But it is to be observed that the productiveness of capital and labour and talent, two hundred and seventy years ago, cannot well be compared with the standards of to-day. Moreover, the results of Champlain's career are insignificant rather in appearance than in reality. The work which he did was in laying foundations, while the superstructure was to be reared in other years and by other hands. The palace or temple, by its lofty and majestic proportions, attracts the eye and gratifies the taste; but its unseen foundations, with their nicely adjusted arches, without which the superstructure would crumble to atoms, are not less the result of the profound knowledge and practical wisdom of the architect. The explorations made by Champlain early and late, the organization and planting of his colonies, the resistance of avaricious corporations, the holding of numerous savage tribes in friendly alliance, the daily administration of the affairs of the colony, of the savages, and of the corporation in

SLAFTER'S TRIBUTE

France, to the eminent satisfaction of all generous and noble-minded patrons, and this for a period of more than thirty years, are proof of an extraordinary continuation of mental and moral qualities. Without impulsiveness, his warm and tender sympathies imparted to him an unusual power and influence over other men. He was wise, modest and judicious in council, prompt, vigorous and practical in administration, simple and frugal in his mode of life, persistent and unyielding in the execution of his plans, brave and valiant in danger, unselfish, honest and conscientious in the discharge of duty. These qualities, rare in combination, were always conspicuous in Champlain, and justly entitle him to the respect and admiration of mankind."

These two quotations are sufficient to supplement the observations that we have made, and there can be no doubt that posterity will forever confirm this opinion of the life and labours of the founder of New France, and that the name of Champlain will never be obliterated from the memory of Canadians.

CHRONOLOGICAL APPENDIX

CHRONOLOGICAL APPENDIX

1567or 1570—Birth of Samuel Champlain.
1598—Champlain makes a voyage to Spain.
1599—Joins an expedition to the West Indies.
1601—Returns from America.
1603—Goes to Canada as lieutenant of Aymar de Chastes, viceroy of New France, explores the river St. Lawrence to Sault St. Louis, and returns the same year.
1604—Follows de Monts' fortune in Acadia as geographer and historian of the expedition; lives on Ste. Croix Island and at Port Royal till the year 1607.
1608—As lieutenant of de Monts, viceroy of New France, Champlain crosses the Atlantic and founds Quebec.
1610—Champlain's expedition against the Iroquois. Leaves for France on September 5th.
1610—Champlain returns to Quebec and goes back to France the same year. His marriage with Hélène Boullé on December 30th, 1610.
1611—Champlain comes again to Quebec; founds Montreal; sails for France on July 20th. The De Monts' company ceases to exist. Comte de Soissons appointed viceroy of New France; dies soon after. The Prince de Condé takes his place and retains Champlain as his lieutenant.

CHAMPLAIN

1613—Champlain sails for Canada and explores the country as far as Allumette Island. Goes to France.

1615—Returns to Quebec with the Récollet Fathers; he goes as far as the Huron country; particulars of these tribes, their customs, manners, etc; Champlain assists them in a war against the Iroquois; follows them and comes back to the Huron country, where he spends the winter.

1616—Leaves for Quebec on May 20th; work of the missionaries in the meantime; meeting of the *habitants* and result of their deliberations; memorandum addressed to the king; Champlain goes to France.

1617—Champlain sails from Honfleur on April 11th for Quebec; Louis Hébert's family accompanies him.

1618—Champlain returns to France. Maréchal de Thémines appointed viceroy *per interim* after Condé's dismissal. Difficulties met by Champlain in 1617; his projects laid before the king. Champlain gains his point and preserves his former position.

1619—Condé sells his commission of viceroy to the Duke of Montmorency; Champlain's new commission of lieutenant of the viceroy. Company of Montmorency formed by the Duke of Montmorency.

1620—Champlain comes back to Quebec with his wife, and stays there till the year 1624.

1621—Champlain receives his instructions from Montmorency and from the king; entitled to help the new company of merchants:

CHRONOLOGICAL APPENDIX

conflict at Quebec between the agents of the old and of the new company; Champlain's firm attitude settles the matter.

1622—The Company of Montmorency rules the country.

1624—Champlain recrosses the ocean, bringing his wife.

1625—Arrival of the Jesuits. Champlain at Tadousac and at Quebec; his intercourse with the Montagnais; the duc de Ventadour named viceroy of New France; Champlain reappointed lieutenant.

1627—Ventadour resigns his office; Cardinal Richelieu organizes the Company of the Hundred Associates; privileges granted to them; Champlain still living at Quebec.

1628—Roquemont sent to Quebec with provisions; his vessels taken by Kirke; Quebec in danger; correspondence between David Kirke and Champlain; the enemy retires; distress at Quebec for the want of food.

1629—Kirke before Quebec; the capitulation; fate of the inhabitants; the missionaries return to France together with Champlain; the last events at Tadousac.

1629-32—Champlain goes to London; negotiations between France and England through the French ambassador; Champlain's visits to the king, and to Cardinal Richelieu; Charles I ready to restore Canada, with certain conditions.

1632—The Treaty of St. Germain-en-Laye terminates the dispute between the two countries, and Quebec is restored to France.

CHAMPLAIN

1632—Arrival at Quebec of the Jesuits; history of their convent since 1626.
1633—Champlain's arrival in Quebec; history of the seminary of Notre Dame des Anges since its foundation; the Jesuits' missions at Miscou Island, in the Maritime Provinces, Acadia, Baie des Chaleurs and Cape Breton. Champlain erects a church at Quebec.
1634—Immigration of French colonists from Perche; Robert Giffard.
1635—Champlain's sickness and death; his wife founds an Ursuline convent at Meaux.

INDEX

INDEX

A

AÏANDACÉ, Huron seminarist, 232
Alexander, Sir William, his mission, 176; his charters, 223
Alix, Marguerite, Champlain's mother-in-law, 66
Alix, Simon, Hélène Boullé's uncle, 66, 170
Anadabijou, chief of the Montagnais, 50, 51, 55, 139
Andehoua, Huron seminarist, 232, 233
Antons, Captain des, 31
Armand-Jean, christian name of Andehoua, 33
Arragon, notary, 66
Atarohiat, Huron seminarist, 233
Ateiachias, Huron seminarist, 233
Atokouchioüani, Huron seminarist, 233
Aubert, Pierre, 170
Aubéri, Father, his labours in Acadia, 236
Aubry, priest, 24
Aumont, Marshal, d', 1

B

BANCROFT, quoted, 87
Barbier, 66
Batiscan, chief of the Montagnais, 68
Beauchesne, clerk, 115
Beaulieu, councillor and almoner to the king, 72
Bellois, Corneille de, 122, 127

Bentivoglio, Guido, papal nuncio, 84
Berkeley, Sir John, commands Porto Rico, 3
Bessabé, chief of the Souriquois, 28
Biencourt, son of Poutrincourt, 38; bound for Port Royol, 68
Bignon, attorney-general, 265
Boileau, attorney, 265
Bonneau, Thomas, 170
Bonnerme, surgeon, accompanies Champlain when Quebec is founded, 41; one of the jury who condemned Jean Duval to death, 43; dies, 46
Bontemps, captain, 252
Boues, Charles de, Récollet, syndic of Canadian Missions, 117, 148
Boulay, his residence at Port Royal, 25
Boullé, Eustache, Champlain's brother-in-law, 134, 136; arrives in 1618, 145; goes to France in 1626, 155, 209; enters the Minim Order, 267
Boullé, Hélène, marries Champlain, 66; comes to Quebec and returns to France, 141; her sojourn at Quebec, 263, 264, 265, 266
Boullé, Nicholas, Champlain's father-in-law, 66; pays his daughter's inheritance to Champlain, 67

289

Bourdon, Jean, comes to Canada, 252; settles at Quebec, 253

Bourioli at Port Royal, 25

Bouthillier, represents the king of France, 220; signs the Treaty of St. Germain-en-Laye, 222

Boyer, Daniel, 122, 123

Brébeuf, Father Jean de, estimates the Huron population, 90; his opinion of the tribe de l'Ours and other Hurons, 92, 93; arrives in New France, 152; assailed by Jacques Michel, 201, 202; leaves for France, 207, 208; returns to Canada, 228; goes to the Huron country, 249

Brûlé, Étienne, with Champlain founding Quebec, 41; sets out for the Ottawa River, 88, 139; interpreter, 143, 144; sent to Three Rivers, 163; betrays Champlain, 194, 202; his excuse, 203; his murder, 246

Bullion, represents France, 220; signs the Treaty of St. Germain-en-Laye, 222

Burel, Friar Gilbert, arrives in Canada, 152; returns to France, 208

Burlamachi, appointed commissioner, 218; sent to France by Charles I, 220, 222

C

CABAHIS, SOURIQUOIS chief, 28

Caën, Emery de, nephew of Guillaume de Caën, 137; vice-admiral of the fleet, 156; leaves Quebec to carry on trade, 157; his character, 182; defends the colony, 183; fights with Kirke, 184; surrenders, 185; proceeds to Quebec, 199; failure of his expedition, 201; tries to secure his goods, 219, 220; comes back to Quebec, 226; banqueted, 228; summoned by Champlain, 249

Caën, Ezechiel de, member of the Company of Rouen, 132, 137

Caën, Guillaume de, member of de Caën's Company, 130, 132; conflicts with Pont-Gravé, 135; his promises, 136; sails for France, 138; present at Cape de la Victoire, 139; visits Quebec and its vicinity, 140; sails for France, 141; returns with the Jesuits, 152; appears before the state council, 155; supports the conduct of the merchants, 157; condones a murderer, 161; his character, 182, 183; his claims, 217, 218, 219

Camaret, Marie, cousin of Champlain, 265

Cananée, Guillaume, navigator, 141

Cartier, Jacques, 13, 22, 23, 28, 29, 34, 35, 45, 52

Casgrain, l'Abbé, his opinion on the site of Champlain's tomb, 261, 262

Castillon, Jacques, one of the Hundred Associates, 168; offers pictures to Quebec church, 240

Caumont, underclerk, 121

Champdoré, carpenter, 22, 34

Champlain, Antoine, father of Samuel, 1

Champlain, Samuel, see chronological appendix, 283-6

INDEX

Charlevoix, Father, quoted, 36, 248, 276

Charton, Friar Francois, 152, 208

Chastes, Aymar de, 7; viceroy of Canada, 8, 9

Chateauneuf, M. de, French ambassador in England, 211; retires from his position, 214; exchanges documents with Fontenay-Mareuil, 216

Chauvin, Pierre, Sieur de la Pierre, at Tadousac, 54; trades in peltry, 63

Chauvin, Pierre de, Sieur de Tontuit, viceroy of Canada, 8, 13, 17, 41, 54

Cheffault, lawyer of Paris, 244

Chenu, Marcel, merchant of Paris, 66

Cherououny, Montagnais chief, 163

Choquillot, notary, 66

Chou, Iuan, Indian friend of Champlain, 181

Clifford, Sir George, 3

Cloutier, Zacharie, comes with Giffard, 252

Cochon, Thomas, merchant, 122

Collier, 56

Condé, Prince de, viceroy of Canada, 73; gives a passport to Captain Maisonneuve, 78; letter from Champlain, 79; contributes to the Récollet fund, 117; conspires against the Queen Regent, 122; discharged from prison, 129

Coton, Father, a Jesuit, 151, 152

Couillard, Elizabeth, a daughter of Guillaume, 225

Couillard, Guillaume, signs the settlers' memorandum, 136; arrives in Canada, 145; his family 146, 184, 195, 196, 208; native of St. Malo, 250

Couillard, Henry, captain of the *Don de Dieu*, 39

Couillard, Jacques, interpreter, 144; submits to Kirke, 185

Cramoisy, Sébastien, one of the Hundred Associates, 171

D

DABLON, SIMON, one of the Hundred Associates, 168

Daniel, Captain, destroys an English fort at Cape Breton, 200, 212

Daniel, Doctor, sent to London, 212, 213

Daniel, Father, director of the Seminary of Notre Dame des Anges, 231, 237

Darache, Captain, trades furs at Tadousac, 40

Darontal, chief of the tribe de la Roche, 103; Champlain's friend, 106

Davost, Father, missionary at Cape Breton, 237

Denys, Charles, settles on the shores of Miramichi River, 237

Denys, Nicholas, founds Fort St. Pierre, 236

Deschamps, surgeon, performs an autopsy at Port Royal, 33

Des Marets, Claude Godet, note on his family, 47, 60; accompanies Champlain's expedition against the Iroquois, 52; arrives from France, 63; present at Cape de la Victoire, 139; Pont-Gravé's grandson, 181

Desportes, Hélène, 146, 208
Desportes, Pierre, 136, 145, 146, 181, 196, 208
Destouches, Eustache Boullé's lieutenant, 155, 209
Dollebeau, Father, perishes at sea, 235
Dolu, intendant of New France, 130, 131, 132, 135
Doughty, A. G., quoted, 168
Duchesne, Adrien, surgeon, 145, 146, 147, 196, 208
Duchesne, Captain, 139
Duchesne, David, one of the Hundred Associates, 168
Du Marché, Father, at Miscou, 234
Dumay, Captain, 133, 134
Dumoulin, shot by an Indian, 164
Du Parc, Jean Godet, his family, 47, 60; commands at Quebec, 64, 68
Du Plessis, Friar Pacifique, 85, 117
Duplessis-Bochart, presents pictures to Quebec church, 240; receives the keys of the fort, 249
Duval, Jean, at Quebec when founded, 41; leads a conspiracy against Champlain, 42; sentenced to death, 43
Du Vernet, interpreter, 144

E

EFFIAT, DUKE D', heads the list of the Hundred Associates, 170
Endemare, Father d', at Cape Breton, 237
Eon, Pierre, member of the Company of St. Malo and Rouen, 122

F

FAILLON, quoted, 207
Féret, 7
Fontenay-Mareuil, French ambassador in England, 214; exchanges documents with Chateauneuf, 216
Foucher, Jean, at Cape Tourmente, 176, 208
Franchise, Sieur de la, 14
Frémin, Father, at the Richibucto mission, 235

G

GAILLON, MICHEL, put to death, 43, 44
Galleran, Father G., 149
Gamache, Marquis de, contributes to the foundation of the Jesuits' College, 228
Gand, see Ré
Garnier de Chapouin, provincial of the Récollets, 85
Gates, Sir Thomas, his letters patent, 223
Gaufestre, Friar Jean, 209
Genestou, at Port Royal, 25
Gesvres, de, 9
Giffard, Robert, surgeon, 164, 174; comes to Canada, 250; receives lands, 251, 252
Godefroy, Jean-Paul, interpreter, 144
Godefroy, Thomas, interpreter, 144
Gomara, Lopez de, 6
Gondoin, Father N., missionary at Miscou, 234
Goudon, Elizabeth, Gervase Kirke's wife, 173
Gravé, François, grandson of Pont-Gravé, 47

INDEX

Gravé, François, Sieur du Pont, accompanies Champlain to Tadousac, 8 ; comes to Canada in 1603, 9 ; proceeds to Sault St. Louis, 13 ; Champlain awaits him at Port au Mouton, 19 ; at Ste. Croix, 32 ; returns to France, 33 ; at Tadousac, 40 ; one of the jury to judge Duval, 43 ; sails for France in 1608, 45 ; arrives at Tadousac, 1609, 47 ; commands the habitation of Quebec, 48 ; his promise to Anadabijou, 51 ; returns to France, 54 ; receives the command of a fur trading vessel, 56, 57 ; trades in peltry, 63 ; sails for France, 64 ; returns to Canada, 106 ; trades at Three Rivers, 121 ; Champlain's rival, 125 ; represents the old company, 133 ; arrives at Quebec, 134 ; his conflict with Guillaume de Caën, 135 ; chief clerk at Quebec, 138 ; at Cape de la Victoire, 139 ; sails for France, 141 ; his illness, 156 ; Champlain reads publicly his commission, 181, 182 ; signs articles of capitulation, 191 ; leaves for Tadousac, 196.

Gravé, Jeanne, 47

Gravé, Robert, son of François, accompanies Champlain on a voyage of discovery along the American coast, 34

Gravé, Vincent, merchant of Rouen, 122

Groux, J., signs a memorandum, 136

Gua, Pierre du, Sieur de Monts, see Monts

Guers, J. B., delegate of the Duke of Montmorency, 121, 133, 134, 136 ; returns to France, 141

Guilbault, merchant of La Rochelle, 236

Guines, Friar Modeste, 115

Guyon, Jean, mason, comes from Perche, 252

H

HALARD, JACQUES, captain, 136

Hébert, Anne, 117

Hébert, Guillaume, 146, 208

Hébert, Guillemette, 146, 208

Hébert, Louis, comes to Quebec with family, 111, 112 ; signs a memorandum, 136 ; his family, 146 ; at Port Royal, 147 ; his death, 148, 250, 251

Hébert, Louise, 146

Hébert, Madame, see Rollet, Marie.

Hersault, Jacques, comptroller of customs at La Rochelle, 265

Hertel, Jacques, interpreter, 144

Hervé, François, merchant of Rouen, 132

Honabetha, Indian chief, 30

Hoüel, Louis, Sieur de Petit-Pré, enters into Champlain's views, 83 ; one of the Hundred Associates, 168, 170

Hubou, Guillaume, 181, 196, 208

Huet, Father Paul, arrives in Canada, 87 ; constructs a chapel at Tadousac, 112

I

INCARNATION, SISTER MARIE DE L', 253, 258

Insterlo, Mathieu d', one of the Company of Rouen, 122, 127
Iroquet, Indian chief, 48

J

Jacques, a Slavonian miner, 32
Jamet, Father Denis, arrives in Canada and celebrates the first mass, 85, 107; goes to France, 111, 112; signs a memorandum, 136
Jeannin, President, 72
Jogues, Father Isaac, 207
Jonquest, Étienne, Hébert's son-in-law, his death, 117; arrives in 1617, 145
Joubert, Captain, 141
Juchereau, Jean, comes with Giffard, 252

K

Kirke, David, intends to make an assault on Quebec, 173; appointed captain of the fleet, 176; writes to Champlain, 177, 178; captures French barques, 179; abandons Quebec, 180; accepts articles of capitulation, 192; visits Quebec, 204; at Tadousac, 205; his pretentions as to de Caën's claims, 217; refuses to pay, 218; dissatisfied with the agreement, 219
Kirke, Gervase, chief of the Kirke family, 173
Kirke, James, son of Gervase, 173
Kirke, John, son of Gervase, 173
Kirke, Louis, resides in Fort St. Louis, 158; writes to Champlain, 188; interviews Father de la Roche, 189, 190; his answer to Champlain, 191, 192; receives the keys of the fort, 195; hoists the English flag, 196; treats Champlain well, 199; his conduct towards the Jesuits, 205
Kirke, Thomas, signs a letter to Champlain, 188; takes part in an interview with Father de la Roche, 189; signs the answer to Champlain, 192; treats Emery de Caën as a pirate, 220

L

Lalemant, Father Charles, quoted, 87; arrives at Quebec, 152; h s letter to the Provincial of the Récollets, 154; comes back to Quebec, 200; abandons Canada, 227; teacher, 229; parish priest, 238, 239
Lalemant, Father Jérôme, 10
Lamontagne, interpreter, 144
La Motte, at Port Royal, 25
L'Ange, Captain, 78
Langlois, Françoise, 146, 208
Langlois, Marguerite, 146, 208
Langlois, Noël, 252
Langoissieux, Pierre, takes the monastic habit, 149; returns to France, 209
La Place, Father de, at Miscou, 234
La Roche d'Aillon, Father, arrives at Quebec, 152; interviews Louis Kirke, 188, 189; relates his interview, 190; returns to France, 208
La Routte, pilot, 52
La Taille, at Quebec when founded, 41
Lattaignant, Gabriel de, one of the Hundred Associates, 168, 170

INDEX

Lauzon, Jean de, 170, 226

Laval, Bishop, 237, 253

Lavalette, a Basque, 59, 60

La Vallée, godfather of young Hurons, 233

Laverdière, antiquarian, 261, 275

Le Baillif, underclerk at Tadousac, 138; arrives in 1623, 144; takes charge of the storehouse, 195; betrays Champlain, 202; his bad character, 204; remains in Canada, 208

Le Baillif, Father George, his Relation of 1633, 87; confers with Champlain, 133; goes to Tadousac, 134; his mission in France, 136; returns to Quebec, 137

Le Borgne, E., takes Fort St. Pierre, 236

Le Caron, Father Joseph, appointed for Canadian missions, 85; proceeds to the Huron country, 88; returns from the Petuneux, 104; receives a visit from Champlain, 106; returns to Quebec, 107; goes to France, 111, 115; goes to Tadousac, 116; his mission at Three Rivers, 117; signs a memorandum, 136; goes to the Huron country, 149; consults with Champlain, 187; leaves for France, 208

Le Clercq, Father C., quoted, 112, 258

Le Faucheur, a Parisian, 174

Legendre, Lucas, merchant of Rouen, 56, 57, 122, 127

Le Jeune, Father, his Relation of 1633, 87; says mass in Hébert's house, 148; writes to his Provincial, 230, 231, 239; informs Madame Champlain that she is free to follow her own desires, 264

Lemaistre, Simon, one of the Hundred Associates, 170

Lemoyne, Father Simon, 208

Le Roy, Marguerite, Champlain's mother, 1

Lesage, Marguerite, Pivert's wife, 146, 208

Lesaige, François, attends when Champlain's marriage settlements are made, 66

Lesaige, Geneviève, attends when Champlain's marriage settlements are made, 66

Lescarbot, Marc, 20, 21, 25, 35; composes a drama, 36; poet and preacher, 37; returns to France, 38

Le Sire, clerk, 138

Lesseps, Ferdinand de, 6

Le Tardif, Olivier, signs a memorandum, 136; interpreter, 144, 208

Le Testu, Captain, arrives at Quebec, 42; entertainment on board of his barque, 43

L'Huillier, Raoul, one of the Hundred Associates, 170

Linschot, quoted, 211

Loquin, clerk, 121, 139

Lormel, Captain de, 252

Lumagne, merchant, 221

Lyonne, Father de, at Nipisiguit, 235

M

MAGNAN, PIERRE; joins an embassy to the Five Nations, 163; murdered, 164

CHAMPLAIN

Mahicanaticouche, chief of the Montagnais, 139, 163; murderer of two Frenchmen, 164, 165
Maisonneuve, captain, 78, 79
Malot, Friar Louis, drowned at sea, 200
Manet, Jean, interpreter, 144
Manitougatche, Indian chief, 187
Marchim, Indian chief, 34
Mariana, Father 153
Marion, Nicholas, captain, 40
Marsolet, Nicholas, present at Quebec in 1608, 41, 143; interpreter, 144; betrays Champlain, 194, 202; his chàracter, 203, 204, 205; remains at Quebec, 208
Martin, Abraham, 145, 146, 147, 196, 208
Martin, Anne, 146
Martin, Charles Amador, priest, 146
Martin, Sir Henry, commissioner, 214
Martin, Marguerite, 146
Martin, Nicholas, commands the *Jonas*, 37
Marye, Anthoine, 66
Massé, Father E., arrives in Canada, 152; objects to the profanation of a chalice, 206; returns to France, 207, 208, 227; comes back, 228
May, Sir Humphrey, commissioner, 214
Membertou, *sagamo* of the Souriquois, 36
Messamouet, captain of the Souriquois 22, 34
Michel, Jacques, insults Father de Brébeuf, 201; his lamented death, 202

Miristou, Montagnais, 159
Mohier, Friar Gervais, 208
Montmagny, Governor, 158
Montmorency, Charles de, admiral of France, 14; succeeds Condé as viceroy of New France, 129; his administration, 130; letter to Champlain, 130, 131; his gift to Guillaume de Caën, 140; meets Champlain at St. Germain-en-Laye, 150; resigns his position of viceroy, 151; put to death, 215
Monts, Pierre du Gua, Sieur de, lieutenant-general in Acadia, 17; forms a company of merchants, 18; his expedition to America, 19, 20; his settlement at Ste. Croix, 21, 22, 23, 24, 25; decides to seek a more suitable place, 26; explores the southern country, 29; the river Gua, 30; determines to try Port Royal as a settlement, 31; returns to France, 32, 33, 34, 35, 36; obtains a new commission, 39, 40; meets Champlain at Fontainebleau, 55; his commission expiring, requests a new one, 56; meets Champlain, 57; attends when Champlain's marriage settlements are made, 66; his interviews with Champlain, 67, 70; holds a conference with the merchants of Rouen, 71; bound to colonize New France with Catholic settlers, 86
Moreau, quoted, 25
Morel, Captain, 112
Motin, his ode to Champlain, 72
Murad, Anthoine de, 66

INDEX

N

NAPAGABISCOU, Indian chief, 176
Natel, Antoine, at Quebec in 1608, 41; acquaints Captain Le Testu with the details of Duval's plot, 43; dies from scurvy, 46
Nesle, Captain de, 252
Nicholas, signs a memorandum, 136
Nicolet, Jean, interpreter, 144
Noël, Pierre, 66
Noüe, Father Anne de, 207, 208, 227
Nouveau, Arnould de, merchant of Rouen, 132
Noyrot, Father, 168, 177, 178, 200, 227

O

OCHATEGUIN, Indian chief, 48; his alliance with Champlain, 55; commands the Hurons, 69; fights against the Iroquois, is wounded, 103
Olbeau, Father Jean d', arrives in Quebec, 85, 88; visits the Bersiamites, 107; celebrates the first jubilee, 114; lays the first stone of the Récollet convent, 148; sees its door closed in 1629, 167
Olmechin, Indian chief, 34
Orville, d', at Ste. Croix, 25
Otis, Charles Pomeroy, translates the *Voyages of Champlain*, 277
Ouanda Koka, Huron chief, 233
Orani, Huron chief wounded in 1615, 103
Overman, finds Champlain's astrolabe, 76

P

PALMA CAYET, VICTOR, 15

Parkman, quoted, 228
Perrault, Father, at Cape Breton, 236, 237
Piat, Father I., goes to France, 141; to the Montagnais, 149 150
Pillet, Charles, murdered, 161, 163
Piraube, Martial, godfather of young Hurons, 233
Pivert, Nicholas, 144, 146, 181, 196, 208
Pont-Gravé, see Gravé, François, Sieur du Pont
Poullain, Father G., comes to Canada, 87, 116; goes to the Nipissing mission, 149
Poutrincourt, Jean de Biencourt, Sieur de, goes to America with de Monts, 19; joins Champlain on a voyage of discovery, 34; plants a cross at Port Fortuné, 35; leaves for France, 38
Prévert, informs Champlain of the existence of a copper mine, 14
Provençal, Captain, Champlain's uncle, 2
Purchas, 15

Q

QUEN, FATHER J. de, second parish priest of Quebec, 238, 239
Quentin, Barthélemy, one of the Hundred Associates, 170
Quentin, Bonaventure, 170
Quentin, Father Claude, superior of the Canadian missions, 234

R

RAGOIS, CLAUDE LE, merchant of Rouen, 132

Ralde, Raymond de la, 138; goes to France, 141; admiral of the fleet, 155; note on his life, 156

Ralleau, de Monts' secretary, 33

Ravenel, Jehan, 66

Raymbault, Father, buried in Champlain's tomb, 262

Razilly, Isaac de, one of the Hundred Associates, 170; ordered to assist Quebec, 200; his commission cancelled, 201, 213

Ré, François de, Sieur Gand, one of the Hundred Associates, 171; a good Catholic, 239; buried in Champlain's tomb, 262

Repentigny, godfather of young Hurons, 233

Reye, Pierre, signs a memorandum, 136; traitor, 194, 202, 204, 208

Richard, Father A., at Richibucto and Miscou, 235

Richer, Jean, interpreter, 144

Roberval, at Charlesbourg Royal, 23

Robin, Guillaume, merchant of Rouen, 132

Robineau, Pierre, one of the Hundred Associates, 170

Roernan, Jehan, 66

Rollet, Marie, widow Hébert, 112, 146, 208

Roquemont, Claude de, 168; commands a fleet for Quebec, 172; meets English vessels, 173; surrenders to David Kirke, 174; his conduct criticized, 175

Rouer, Hercule, 66

Rouvier, underclerk, 121, 135

Rozée, Jean, one of the Hundred Associates, 170; merchant of Rouen, 244

Russell, A. J., 76

S

SAGARD-THÉODAT, Friar Récollet, at Cape de la Victoire, 139; returns to France, 141; goes to the Huron country, 149; quoted, 193

Santein, clerk, 138

Satouta, Huron seminarist, 232

Savignon, Huron boy accepted as hostage, 63; goes to Sault St. Louis, 68; brother of Tregouaroti, Indian chief, 69

Schoudon, Indian chief, 32

Séguier, Bishop of Meaux, agrees to the founding of an Ursuline convent at Meaux, 266

Slafter, Reverend E. B., quoted, 277, 278, 279

Soissons, comte de, appointed viceroy of New France, 72, 73; his death, 73

Soubriago, General, 2

Sourin, at Ste. Croix Island, 25

Stuart, James, Scottish fisherman, erects a fort on Cape Breton, 200

T

TEOUATIRHON, Huron seminarist, 232

Tessouat, chief of the Algonquins, 75, 76, 77

Thémines, Maréchal de, appointed viceroy of New France, 122, 123

Thierry-Desdames, appointed captain at Miscou, 121; note on his life, 138; 173, 181, 209

INDEX

Tregatin, Indian chief, 176
Tregouaroti, Huron Chief, 69
Troyes, François de, merchant of the Company of Rouen, 132
Trublet, Pierre, merchant of St. Malo, 122
Tsiko, Huron seminarist, 232, 233
Tuffet, Jean, merchant of Bordeaux, 170
Turgis, Father C., at Miscou, 234

V

VANELLY, merchant, 221
Vendremur, Corneille de, clerk, 204, 209
Ventadour, duc de, receives the commission of viceroy of New France, 151; resigns the office, 168
Verrazano, 211
Verger, Father du, Récollet, 83
Vermeulle, Louis, merchant, 122, 127

Verton, Pierre de, merchant 132
Viel, Father N., at Cape de la Victoire, 139; goes to the Huron country, 149
Vieux-Pont, Father de, 200, 237
Vignau, Nicholas du, interpreter, 74, 75, 77, 144
Vigne, Captain de la, 141
Villemenon, intendant of admiralty, 123, 130, 132, 135
Vimont, Father, drowned at sea, 200, 237
Vitelleschi, Father, general of the Jesuits, 228

W

WAKE, SIR ISAAC, English ambassador to France, 215; commissioner, 218, 219, 220; signs the Treaty of St. Germain-en-Laye, 222

CANADIAN UNIVERSITY PAPERBOOKS

1. *The Canadian Identity* by W. L. Morton.
2. *The Fur Trade in Canada* by Harold A. Innis.
3. *Rideau Waterway* by Robert Legget.
4. *The Politics of Education* by Frank MacKinnon.
5. *Our Living Tradition* edited by C. T. Bissell.
6. *Essays in Canadian Economic History* by Harold A. Innis.
7. *The Bruce Beckons* by W. Sherwood Fox.
8. *The Renaissance and English Humanism* by Douglas Bush.
9. *Democracy in Alberta: Social Credit and the Party System* by C. B. Macpherson.
10. *The Birth of Western Canada* by George F. G. Stanley.
11. *Rhythm in the Novel* by E. K. Brown.
12. *Between the Red and the Rockies* by Grant MacEwan.
13. *Champlain* by N. E. Dionne.

www.ingramcontent.com/pod-product-compliance
Lightning Source LLC
Chambersburg PA
CBHW031407290426
44110CB00011B/291